DIDEROT

Jacques le fataliste

Geoffrey Bremner

Lecturer in French,
Department of Romance Languages, University College of Wales,
Aberystwyth

Grant & Cutler Ltd
1985

© Grant & Cutler Ltd
1985
ISBN 0 7293 0186 9

I.S.B.N. 84-599-0408-3

DEPÓSITO LEGAL: V. 321 - 1985

Printed in Spain by
Artes Gráficas Soler, S.A., Valencia
for
GRANT & CUTLER LTD
11 BUCKINGHAM STREET, LONDON W.C.2

Contents

References

References to the text of *Jacques le fataliste* (by page numbers in brackets) are to the edition by Yvon Belaval (Paris, Gallimard, Collection Folio, 1973). As well as a useful introduction and notes, this volume contains an outline of Diderot's life.

References to works listed in the Bibliographical Guide at the end of this volume give the number of the work in italics followed by the page-numbers, thus: *8*, pp.73-81.

1. *Accepting* Jacques le fataliste *on its own Terms*

However much people may enjoy *Jacques le fataliste* at a first reading, their first *critical* reaction is almost certain to be one of confusion. The next reaction, since it is the duty of most readers of the book to 'make something of it' for examination purposes, is to try to reduce the confusion to some kind of order. The result, in the case of *Jacques* more than with most books, is to destroy its very essence, not to speak of any pleasure we might hope to find in it. For *Jacques* is perhaps one of the best examples there is of a work which invites us to take it as it is, to accept it on its own terms. It sets out to be different, perversely refusing to provide us with the things we normally expect to find in a story. What we must not do therefore is to try to categorize it, to tabulate it in some way, or simplify it to make it easier to follow. This would involve missing the whole point, for there *is*, of course, a point.

Our first aim must be to abandon the assumptions which we are so often tempted to bring to the study of a serious work of literature, the attempt to discover the 'real' subject of the book beneath (in this case) the jokes, the verbiage, the distracting interventions of the narrator, the constant introduction of seemingly irrelevant anecdotes and so on. If the book is worth anything, then it is precisely here, in all this confusion, that the point will be found. There is in almost all of us an automatic tendency to reduce works of art to some straightforward 'message', to bring them down to the level of our ordinary lives, but the true interest of any worthwhile work of art lies in its differentness from everyday experience, its uniqueness. We need to become receptive to the distinctive flavour of a work, and in the case of *Jacques le fataliste* the flavour is very distinctive indeed.

I have said that we must try to cast off the set of prejudices with which we tend to approach a serious work of literature, and perhaps the best way to do this where *Jacques* is concerned is to replace them, initially at least, with another set, those we bring to the reading of an undemanding novel, a story read for pure entertainment. These are in fact the prejudices and assumptions which Diderot is attacking, for the reading public of his time had an ever increasing range of novels at its disposal, and had inevitably developed a certain number of expectations from the genre. In this sense *Jacques* is unorthodox in its intention as well as its form; Diderot certainly did not regard it as a 'literary' text, and would no doubt have been amazed to discover that it now figures on the literature syllabus of many universities and is the subject of much discussion amongst academics.

Many of the things which an eighteenth-century reader expected from a story were of course the same as we expect ourselves. Then as now, side by side with the more serious readers were those who wanted an undemanding, escapist 'read'. But more so than today, novelists tried to *combine* the elements of seriousness and entertainment in their books: there was not the distinction we know today between literary novels and those written for pure entertainment. Every novel-reader, therefore, would be accustomed to expecting a good story-line with clearly delineated characters involved in interesting and exciting events. They would demand, as we often do, a story in which they could become totally absorbed, and which would hold their interest without ever reminding them that it was in fact pure invention.

In addition, eighteenth-century readers would usually have had a further, more rigorous requirement: they would have wanted not just a story which offered total absorption, but one which had all the appearance of having actually taken place. It is as though the boundary-line between fact and fiction, at least where the novel was concerned, was more obscurely drawn. The realistic novel, as it developed in the late seventeenth century and in the eighteenth, had justified its existence as a new form of reading which contained a guarantee of truth to real life, and this is one of the assumptions which Diderot is attacking: that what we read in novels is the truth.

At this point the best way to proceed is to look at the text itself and try to achieve that delicate balance between relaxation and receptivity which any good piece of writing requires and deserves. In fact the first few pages provide, as we should expect, a number of useful pointers as to how we should read the text. The opening lines could be — indeed have been — commented upon endlessly, but for the moment it will be enough to say two things: firstly, that the narrator is airily and rather impatiently dismissing the questions we should like to have answered about the two people named in the title, questions which would be answered without being asked in the average novel. The second point is that these questions, and their unsatisfactory answers, destroy the comfortable relationship which we, the readers, like to have with a story. Where do we stand? It seems that we are being made fun of by the narrator. And there are two further uncertainties: is the narrator meant to be Diderot himself or an invented figure within the book itself? And in the same way, is it we who are being mocked as readers or another invented figure, the 'typical reader' perhaps? There seem to be no answers to these questions either, and the whole effect is to disorientate us.

When we do get something resembling a proper answer, to the question 'Que disaient-ils?', it is simply a popular cliché, expressing a fatalistic attitude. Moreover, it is not even Jacques's own idea, but one he got from his 'capitaine', whose identity is not explained. Nevertheless, his master answers (for we now find ourselves reading a dialogue) with apparent approval, as he also does to Jacques's second quotation from the captain, which is even more banal than the first. If we had hoped for some enlightenment on the subject of fatalism, we now see that we are unlikely to get it from Jacques. But in any case Jacques has been distracted from his reflexions, or so it appears until his master realizes — perhaps more quickly than we do — that the 'cabaretier et son cabaret' have a distant causal connection with the particular bullet which was meant for Jacques, and which itself set off a chain of events, the most significant of which is a love affair.

This immediately arouses the master's interest, as, presumably, it does ours, but Jacques, as is proper to a fatalist, is not sure whether the moment for recounting his love-story has arrived or not. On the master's insistence he begins, or rather we are told he begins, for dialogue has now given place to narrative, Jacques's words to those of the narrator, who now describes the events which prevent Jacques continuing his story. And so our hopes, which we share with Jacques's master, that we might be about to hear an actual story are immediately dashed by an outside event: Jacques gets lost, and is beaten by his master. But even the possibility that this setback might be put right is temporarily denied us by the narrator, who now steps out of his role and addresses us directly. We are thus prevented from enjoying the two satisfactions we look for: absorption in the story, since Jacques is prevented from telling it, and the conviction that the story has a basis in reality, since the narrator goes on to suggest a number of possible continuations for it.

None of these, however, is allowed to materialize. At dawn the next day we are back with our travellers, or would be, if our representative reader had not imprudently annoyed the narrator by asking 'Et où allaient-ils?'. Now we are given a choice: either the subject of the journey, or Jacques's love-story...'Ils allèrent quelque temps en silence', runs the next sentence, and the silence seems necessary both for Jacques and his master and for the narrator and ourselves to calm down after our respective disagreements: then Jacques is allowed, for a brief period, to tell his story.

Let us pause here for a moment to take stock. If we were looking for a story, then we have not got very far. Indeed it is not altogether clear whether the real story, if in fact there is such a thing, is the journey of Jacques and his master or the story told by Jacques. Nor can we be sure whether the stories are being told for their own sake, to satisfy curiosity, or to illustrate some point about fatalism, since Jacques so frequently alludes to it. However that may be, the story-telling is only part of the total picture, since it is interrupted by the comments of Jacques and his master, by events, and by the comments of the narrator himself, and this will to a large extent be the pattern of the whole book. We, the readers, are constantly being forced to readjust our sights, to become now more, now less, distanced from the story (assuming, that is, that we can decide which is the story). We seem at certain moments to be almost part of the action, as I suggested in the previous paragraph; at others we are sharing the viewpoint of the narrator.

Obviously there is no point in resolutely ignoring these difficulties in order to do what Diderot (or the narrator) implies we really want to do, that is to follow the journey, or Jacques's love-story, from beginning to end. In either case we should be left with a very short story indeed. On the other hand, we should not try to remain constantly at a critical distance from these and the many other stories in the book. In fact, unless we are very tense and earnest readers, this is quite impossible, for the stories we *are* finally allowed to hear, even with all the interruptions from one source or another, are often very funny and sometimes very absorbing. We should not forget the amount of sheer enjoyment the book offers just on this anecdotic level.

We have for example the various incidents which accompany the two men's journey: the bandits in the inn, Jacques's return to the place where they had spent the night to retrieve his master's watch and his own purse, the antics of the executioner's horse; or the various events of Jacques's love-life: Justine, the 'initiation' by *dames* Marguerite and Suzon, the rather more decorous and touching relationship with Denise; and of course the stories told by Jacques, his master, the narrator himself, and the people they meet on the way. That these stories and incidents are enjoyable should go without saying, but so much has been written (and will be written here) about the structure of the book, about the complex scaffolding which supports the various characters and stories, that anyone who approaches *Jacques* as a student is in danger of seeing the book simply as a problem, a complicated web to be disentangled, and not as, among other things, a series of well-told stories which can be enjoyed for their own sake.

Needless to say, there is a point in all these stories, and I shall be quoting some of them as examples of such points later, but the first point is that, being enjoyable, they do involve us. One of the elements that constitute the quality of a good book is that the enjoyment it gives at the same time contributes to our understanding of it. In the same way a bad book contains a number of elements which simply amuse, or titillate, without offering anything beyond that immediate pleasure. Part of the humour and depth of *Jacques le fataliste* lies in the fact that it seems at first sight to present us with a number of incidents which have nothing to do with the story, no function beyond the amusement they provide; but a further effect they have is to illustrate Diderot's point simply by the fact that they hold our attention: they involve us, despite ourselves and despite the interruptions provoked by the narrator.

For, as I have said, a dominant feature of this novel is that we are constantly being shuttled backwards and forwards between involvement and detachment; our perspective on the events is constantly being shifted. An early example of this is the anecdote about the poet of Pondicherry (pp.71-73). The narrator has broken off his story of the surgeon's negotiations with Jacques's host and hostess to reflect on the need for the details of a story to be interesting as well as true, and is thus reminded of the poet he sent to Pondicherry. The reader's curiosity is immediately aroused, and he insists on hearing it, despite the narrator's attempts to pursue the story of the surgeon. The reader wins, the story is told, and the narrator then goes back to Jacques's story. The story of the poet is in fact both amusing and instructive; it also happens to be true (*1*, note 47, p.398) and is thus an example of the truth being interesting. But at the same time its overt message is that writers who feel the urge to write will go on doing so whether anyone is interested or not. And a further lesson which should have come home to the reader is that he (the reader) is quite prepared to abandon a story which he had earlier been impatient to hear (Jacques's love-story) and become involved in another which sounds more interesting. What then are we finally to make of the story of the poet of Pondicherry? The answer must be, I think, that we should confine ourselves to these reflections and then suspend our critical judgement until the total picture becomes clearer. In a long and complex work like *Jacques le fataliste* no clear-cut 'message' is likely to emerge from a single incident.

What we do find is that the theme of involvement and

detachment recurs in a variety of forms throughout the novel. In addition to the example just quoted of the reader's willingness to become detached from one story and involved in another, we have a whole range of cases where the narrator interrupts his own story, and where the reader interrupts the narrator (and I shall return to some of these later in a slightly different context); a parallel range in which the master interrupts Jacques, and vice-versa; and, resulting from some of these interruptions, a series of reflections, discussions and stories which break the narrative sequence and at the same time throw light on the questions raised by the novel.

Some of these are fairly clear in their intention, like the anecdote about Aesop (p.83). This is introduced to prove the irrelevance of the reader's repeated demand to know where Jacques and his master are going, and illustrates the impossibility of knowing such a thing. Of course there is more to it than this. Diderot knows, and we know, that the author is perfectly able to tell us where they are going if he wants to, since, despite his protests that he is telling the truth, he is in fact making it all up. This tongue-in-cheek, teasing approach to the reader is part of the tone of the book.

The word that perhaps best describes all these interventions and interruptions is 'inconsequential'. Their nature and timing is completely unpredictable, and their connection with the surrounding text is sometimes clear, as in the case of the Aesop story, sometimes less clear, as in the Pondicherry story, and sometimes very obscure, as for example with the funeral oration delivered by Jacques's master when Jacques is bewailing the supposed death of his captain (pp.84-85). Of course, an explanation of a sort is eventually given to Jacques, who is as mystified as we are: it is that the absurdity of the oration, its total unsuitability to the circumstances, have distracted Jacques from his grief. As his master triumphantly explains (p.85): 'il m'a paru que vous m'écoutiez avec attention tandis que je lisais'. Once again we have a case of involvement in one thing replacing involvement in another, with the implication that any inconsistencies in what the master (or the narrator) says are matched by the inconsistency of the listener.

Over and above the points which may emerge from them, the
cumulative effect of all these inconsequential incidents is to
produce a climate in which we never know what to expect, and
where successive events and utterances can never be relied upon
to have any connection with each other. Before discussing this
theme further it will be useful to examine one set of devices
which Diderot uses to produce this effect, and of which the
funeral oration is an example. These devices can generally be
described as those where Diderot moves beyond the story or the
immediate subject of discussion to refer, usually in a humorous
way, to other areas of experience.

Parody, allusion, cliché.

The short speech delivered by Jacques's master is a parody of
the style of the funeral oration, and there are frequent examples
of parody in *Jacques*, or else of allusion to other works or
genres. We have direct comparisons with other works, like that‾
between Jacques and his master and Don Quixote and Sancho
Panza (p.99), or (p.138) the parallel between Goldoni's *Bourru
bienfaisant* and the incident between the host at the inn and the
peasant, a·parallel which induces Diderot to suggest a better
treatment of Goldoni's subject. The effect of these comparisons
is to invite us to see the characters in a broader, literary context,
again encouraging a critical detachment in the reader, and,
beyond that, conferring an ambiguous status on characters and
events, so that we are not sure whether to see them as examples
of truth or as literary creations.

On a rather different level, but with a similar effect, is
Jacques's master's comment on the story of Madame de La
Pommeraye (p.196). If there is any story in which we are likely
to have become emotionally involved, it is this one, and
Jacques's comment, that 'le marquis des Arcis fut un des
meilleurs maris et eut une des meilleures femmes qu'il y eût au
monde' (p.195) is the sort of conclusion we should like to have
for it. But then we are thrown off balance by his master's
observations, a parody of the rather pedantic literary criticism
of the period, in which the character of Mademoiselle Duquênoi

is condemned, not on moral grounds, but for reasons of psychological inconsistency. 'Quand on introduit un personnage sur la scène, il faut que son rôle soit un'; and so the hostess is condemned for having offended against the rules of Aristotle, Horace, Vida and Le Bossu. Our perspective on the story is altered, and if our first reaction is to be amused at Jacques's master's blinkered subservience to traditional critical method, our second might be to consider that he is, in a sense, right. One of the points of the Pommeraye story is its inconsequential outcome, the refusal of life to conform to the rational demands of literature; and of course this is a point which has a bearing on *Jacques* as a whole.

There are many other examples of parody, and here a word of warning is necessary. Parody is only recognizable as such if we know what is being parodied, and many of those who come to *Jacques le fataliste* without a wide knowledge of eighteenth-century life and literature will not always be able to recognize cases of parody. For this reason alone anyone who wants to get the best out of *Jacques* should have access to a well annotated edition. Sometimes of course the parody is obvious. For example, nobody could miss the fact that the hostess's pronouncement (p.209) on Jacques's dispute with his master is a parody of legal jargon. Sometimes Diderot draws our attention to it, as when Jacques (p.298) mutters between his teeth: 'Tu me la payeras ce maudit portrait', after his master has given us a literary portrait of the widow who lives near Desglands. But even here it might be only the later allusions to the subject (pp.301; 302) which would indicate that the character portrait was a commonplace of contemporary literature.

Standard features of the literature of a period can come very close to cliché, and here again we may fall into the trap of taking for serious comment what is merely a repetition of a popular commonplace. (In fact some quite reputable critics have fallen into this trap.) For example, when the narrator is teasing the reader about where Jacques and his master spent the night, he offers a number of alternatives, among which are: 'qu'ils soient réfugiés chez des moines mendiants, où ils furent mal logés et mal repus pour l'amour de Dieu; qu'ils aient été accueillis dans la maison d'un grand, où ils manquèrent de tout ce qui est nécessaire, au milieu de tout ce qui est superflu'; and a little further on: 'qu'ils se soient enivrés d'excellents vins, aient fait grande chère et pris une indigestion bien conditionnée dans une riche abbaye de Bernardins' (pp.57-58).

There is a temptation to take the first and last possibilities as a passing dig at the monastic orders, and the second as directed against the aristocracy. One could add these to the other quite numerous jibes at monks, priests, nobles and so on, and turn *Jacques le fataliste* into a satire on the church and aristocracy. But even if these comments do have a mild satirical effect, we need to know that they are all part of the stock-in-trade of the social criticism of the time, and would no doubt be recognized as such by a contemporary reader. Diderot is simply offering a number of clichés for our amusement, and as a satire, more probably, on the novels of the period; perhaps even on the banality of our own expectations.

Jacques's master, in particular, has a tendency to indulge unexpectedly in rhetorical flights, as when, suddenly convinced of Jacques's imminent death (p.93), he tells him to put his affairs in order, or when (p.110) he describes the condition of the philosopher in this world. The first example can obviously not be taken at face value, but it is probably less obvious that the second cannot either, for here again we have a set of observations with which any reasonably educated person could be familiar. It is probably true to say that there are very rarely any original observations in *Jacques le fataliste*. The originality lies elsewhere. From Jacques's very first remark (p.35), quoted from his captain as though it were a gem of wisdom, 'que tout ce qui nous arrive de bien et de mal ici-bas était écrit là-haut', to his final one (p.330), 's'il est écrit là-haut que tu seras cocu, Jacques, tu auras beau faire, tu le seras' (which at least shows that he is consistent in his basic belief), the novel is full of platitudes, references to stock points of view and examples of conventional wisdom. Sometimes we have to rely on our knowledge or perception to see this; at other times the characters make fun of themselves, as in Jacques's comment on the Lisbon earthquake (p.81); or else the narrator makes fun of them, as when Jacques and his master argue about women (pp.55-56), or about one of the central themes, destiny (p.41): 'Vous concevez, lecteur, jusqu'où je pourrais pousser cette conversation sur un sujet dont on a tant parlé, tant écrit depuis deux mille ans, sans en être d'un pas plus avancé'.

Perhaps the best example of this technique is the passage where we do seem to be hearing some solid, serious opinions, when the narrator is reflecting on the popular interest in executions, and goes on to speak of Jacques's philosophy (pp.216-18). Certainly it looks as though we are at last being given something to get our teeth into, something which might (to change the metaphor) throw some light on the text as a whole, and in a sense this is true. Moreover, anyone who is at all familiar with Diderot's writings will recognize close similarities with his views on determinism, materialism and so on. But as always Diderot removes any feeling of security we might have by telling us that all these views come from elsewhere. In the first place we learn that the observations on public hangings are not the narrator's own, but Jacques's: 'Tout ce que je vous débite là, lecteur, je le tiens de Jacques, je vous l'avoue...' (p.217), and then we are reminded that Jacques's views are in reality those of his captain, who himself got them from reading Spinoza (p.218).

It seems to be Diderot's intention to remove the ground from under our feet whenever we think we are getting somewhere. Many readers will find this irritating. Indeed, the apparent lack of seriousness with which Diderot treats almost the whole novel for a long time prevented it from being appreciated, and it is only during the last thirty or forty years that *Jacques* has really drawn the serious attention of critics and scholars. Before that, both the inconsequentiality of its structure and the apparent frivolity of most of its subject-matter led most readers to dismiss it as a piece of light-hearted (and not very creditable) distraction on Diderot's part. In fact Diderot seems to have foreseen this reaction in his address to the reader on the subject of obscenity (pp.260-62), where he makes the reader say: 'Et votre *Jacques* n'est qu'une insipide rapsodie de faits, les uns réels, les autres imaginés, écrits sans grâce et distribués sans ordre'. And by the standards of most literature of the time (with the partial exception of Sterne's *Tristram Shandy*, to which Diderot paid homage by plagiarizing it), indeed by the standards of literature in general, this criticism is justified.

To enlarge on this comment we might also say that the expressions of opinion, and the literary and rhetorical passages, have a similar place in this 'rapsodie de faits...réels' and 'imaginés', for the total effect is that we are left with nothing to rely upon. Nothing that is said carries the author's guarantee of verifiable truth, nor the status of a point of view of which he would like to persuade us. Statements and opinions, like the incidents of the story, and the anecdotes which interrupt it, follow one upon another without apparent order or justification. A similar point emerges from the narrator's frequent reminders (which I shall deal with more fully in the next chapter) that he is not writing a story but telling us the truth. This again is another case of teasing, since we are well aware that the story of Jacques and his master (though not some of the anecdotes) is fictional. Diderot is anxious to blur the distinction we usually make between fact and fiction, and to suggest, presumably, that if we are looking for factual truth, we should look elsewhere. And this is surely the point of all the play with parody, cliché, literary styles, true facts and false ones, references to real people and fictional ones: that what Diderot is trying to tell us is to be found on another level.

One of the best clues to the level at which we might find this truth is in fact contained in the passage with which this discussion began. The account of Jacques's third-hand philosophy of determinism concludes with yet another example of the inconsequential (p.218). 'D'après ce système, on pourrait imaginer que Jacques ne se réjouissait, ne s'affligeait de rien; cela n'était pourtant pas vrai. Il se conduisait à peu près comme vous et moi.' Often, we learn, 'il était inconséquent comme vous et moi', sometimes following his principles, sometimes not. Jacques, then, like ourselves, and like the book through which he exists, is 'inconséquent', and his inconsistency lies in the fact that his actions are not always in keeping with his beliefs and principles. Diderot is pointing us towards reading the book, at one level at least, as a commentary on the gulf between beliefs and actions, or theory and experience. And it should be recalled that this subject is very much a preoccupation of eighteenth-century thinkers, and also a central theme of another unorthodox work of the period, Voltaire's *Candide*.

Consistency is of course doubly difficult for Jacques because of the particular nature of his convictions. To believe that everything that happens is foreordained inevitably leads one into a hopeless circle of contradictions when one tries to apply this belief to one's actions, and the sort of muddle it can produce is illustrated when Jacques tells the story of his generosity to the woman who broke her pitcher of oil (pp.118-19). Jacques's master has become so incensed that 'celui qui a écrit le grand rouleau' should allow Jacques, after his act of generosity, to be attacked and beaten by bandits, that he becomes involved in the story, almost imagining himself there, so that Jacques has to bring him back to reality: 'Mon maître, rassurez-vous, me voilà'. There follows a lament by Jacques on his inability to find a consistent attitude to life. Some of it, typically, is expressed in a parody of poetic style: 'Nous marchons dans la nuit au-dessous de ce qui est écrit là-haut, également insensés dans nos souhaits, dans notre joie et dans notre affliction' (p.119), a style, moreover, which is quite out of keeping with what we know of Jacques. The rest is a despairing account of the way in which he cannot help reacting to fate as though it might have been different, as if there were something to be done about it.

This sequence in one way reflects the pattern of the whole book. Jacques's master gets caught up in his servant's story to the point of inveighing against the author of Jacques's destiny, as though he could do something about what has already been decided. The whole attitude is caricatured when he even forgets present reality and transports himself into the past: 'Que vas-tu devenir?' Jacques himself describes a similar predicament regarding his attitude to his own life, and the comedy of the situation, helped by the use of parody, encourages us to see Jacques not as the tragic individual for which, at that moment, he takes himself, but as a rather exaggerated example of a situation in which we all find ourselves. Not only does Jacques's life stand in the same relationship to him as his story does to his listening master, but we, the readers, are encouraged to take a similar view of ourselves.

Similar hints are planted throughout the book, like the passage I quoted earlier (p.218), where we are invited to compare our own inconsistency with that of Jacques, or another where our own role is compared with that of Jacques's master (p.83): 'Homme passionné comme vous, lecteur; homme importun comme vous, lecteur; homme questionneur comme vous, lecteur'. As we gather up these clues to the way we should read the text, the whole situation of Jacques and his master becomes a reflection, in caricature, of our own attitudes to literature, and, more importantly, life. The inconsistencies of the story reflect the inconsistencies of life, and of our own attitude towards it, and this relationship is reflected within the story by the relationship between Jacques and his master, which I shall analyse more fully in Chapter 3. Diderot seems to be exploiting our attitude to a fiction (*Jacques le fataliste*) to provide a commentary on our attitude to life itself, and he does it principally by destroying the distinction we habitually make between fact and fiction, real experience and narrative.

2. Truth and Fiction

For want of a better word, *Jacques le fataliste* is usually referred to as a novel. This is ironic, since Diderot so often insists that what we are reading is not a novel, but the truth. Obviously he does not mean by 'truth' a series of events which actually happened. He is simply inviting us, by one of his favourite methods, teasing, to reflect on our own conception of truth, whether in life or in the novel. This is one of the areas where it is useful to have some background knowledge, in this case knowledge of the development and status of the novel in the eighteenth century. As far as possible I have tried, and shall try, to deal with *Jacques le fataliste* purely in terms of itself, with a minimum of reference to the contemporary scene. There are of course various points of view on this question, ranging from those who hold that it is always desirable to approach a text for itself, in historical isolation, to those who would claim that it is impossible to appreciate a work without the fullest possible knowledge of the historical climate in which it was produced. This is no place to embark on a discussion of this problem, but the principle I am adopting is to mention historical background only when it may help to avoid misunderstanding.

The novel in France grew out of two traditions, both dating back to the seventeenth century. One was the pastoral novel, which we should now call a 'romance', and of which Honoré d'Urfé's early seventeenth-century *L'Astrée* is the best-known example. Its main subject was love, and it was set in idyllic, pastoral surroundings. As such it was both immensely popular and at the same time condemned for its escapism and unreality. The other tradition was that of the memoir-novel, originally modelled on actual memoirs, mostly written by participants in the Fronde, the mid-seventeenth-century civil war. This genre became very popular in the early eighteenth century and was sharply distinguished from the romance by its comparatively realistic subject-matter, usually based on recent history. Many of these novels claimed to be the authentic memoirs of real people.

The two traditions often merged in individual novels, and the genre quickly developed other forms and explored other subject-matter, particularly travel, adventure and sex, but the two rather contradictory traditions persisted in people's minds: one, of the novel as a distortion of reality, the other, of a genre which came too close to reality for comfort. In either case it was seen as a potentially corrupting influence, especially on young people. For this reason novelists regularly insisted, in their prefaces, and sometimes in the text, on the morally uplifting nature of their stories, as well as claiming that what they were offering the public was the truth. Both claims served, in their different and rather contradictory ways, as a justification for morally doubtful subject-matter. This partly explains why the novel, despite its immense and growing popularity, never in the eighteenth century achieved the status of literature, never acquired the respectability of poetry and the drama. These and other aspects of the history of the novel are fully treated by Mylne and Showalter (*6* and *7*).

We need to bear in mind these facts, which conditioned the contemporary perception of the novel as a genre, when we read the comments the narrator makes on his own story in *Jacques le fataliste*. One of his most frequent claims is that he is not behaving like a novelist, in other words not letting his imagination run away with him and involving Jacques and his master in all kinds of wild adventures (e.g. pp.36, 38, 47, 49 and so on). Instead, he says, we are going to hear the truth, or something very like it. 'Celui qui prendrait ce que j'écris pour la vérité, serait peut-être moins dans l'erreur que celui qui le prendrait pour une fable' (p.47). The distinction made here is between 'vérité' and 'fable', 'fable' meaning not exactly a fable in the modern English sense, but simply a story which is a product of the imagination.

The matter is looked at in more detail, and from a rather different angle, a few pages later (pp.49-50). The narrator first of all tells us what temptation he is resisting in not blowing up the dispute between the surgeons into a fist-fight. But such things, he says, we can find 'dans les romans, dans la comédie ancienne et dans la société'. And he is reminded of the need to amuse his reader, as well as tell him the truth, by a parallel between the host's 'que diable faisait-elle à sa porte?' and Molière's 'Qu'allait-il faire dans cette galère?' The implication seems to be that in *Jacques* we are hearing the truth, if necessary at the expense of being amused. But we are not, as we next discover, hearing the whole truth, for the narrator is being selective about Jacques's story, which, if it included every detail, would be likely to send us to sleep. Nor shall we hear all the gory details of the operation on Jacques's knee.

But now we come to an item which the narrator insists on our hearing, 'ce que je ne vous laisserais pas ignorer pour tout l'or du monde', an obvious hint that we should pay close attention. The key incident is where Jacques's master, having rejected Jacques's claim that a knee injury is supremely painful, himself falls and hurts his knee. The incident is amusing of course — it serves Jacques's master right. It also makes him realize the painful truth about a knee injury, and, more importantly, leads to a discussion, of a kind, about our powerlessness to comprehend other people's pain unless we have felt a similar pain ourselves. In itself, this is hardly a profound observation, but taken in conjunction with the preceding passages it does, I think, tell us something about Diderot's aims.

He is not, he implies, trying to convey an exciting picture, full of lively, unusual events, nor a witty dialogue, full of memorable *bons mots*, nor a crudely realistic description, with nothing left out. But what he offers us instead is not another kind of truth, but a commentary on truth and the problem of its communication. By moving from a descriptive to a reflective mode he invites us to ponder the question ourselves (p.50): 'je voudrais bien savoir' whether Jacques did not feel a little pleasure mingled with the distress at his master's discomfiture. 'Une autre chose, lecteur, que je voudrais bien que vous me dissiez', is whether Jacques's master did not feel more ashamed than physically hurt. The whole question is seen as a complex one, and is summed up, not in a final clear-cut conclusion, but by Jacques's despairing cry: 'Ah, si je savais dire comme je sais penser!' After which he plunges confusedly into 'une métaphysique très subtile et peut-être très vraie' (p.51) on the notion of pain and our reactions to it.

One could interpret this passage, and the elements which go to make it up, in a variety of ways, but this study is not intended to offer any kind of definitive interpretation, even if such a thing were possible. What I am suggesting is that we should avoid the tendency to concentrate on the separate elements in isolation, because they acquire their significance only through their relationship to a whole sequence of elements. This is not to say that the individual references, to Molière, or to extreme realism, and so on, are not of interest in themselves, as are the notes in the Droz edition (*1*), which reveal how much of Diderot's thought and writings have gone into *Jacques*, but the important thing is to keep one's sense of proportion, to try to keep the whole picture in mind. More than most books, *Jacques le fataliste* needs to be considered in a broad perspective, in which every element casts some light on the whole picture. This is a lot to ask, of course, and perhaps it is ultimately impossible, but the effort must be made if one wants to get the best out of it.

To pursue the example a little further: if we bear in mind, as we read on, that the section I have just discussed is about the communication of truth, in this case intimate personal truth, then we can see a link with the next section, where Jacques's host and hostess also prove their inability to understand each other's truth. The man cannot understand his wife's sympathy for Jacques; she cannot understand his concern about their poverty, especially when he wants to give her another baby; but they finally reach some sort of sympathy with each other as they make love. Whereas the earlier passage was about our failure to sympathize with other people's pain, this one is about our failure to understand another's desires and worries, until, in this case, the desires momentarily become the same, just as Jacques's master's pain momentarily becomes the same as Jacques's.

Once again we have a passage which is illuminated by what went before and in its turn illuminates it. If we now remember that the original discussion was about the problems of writing, particularly descriptive writing, then the whole sequence has something to tell us about this too, for much of what Diderot wants to say is conveyed not in description, but in conversation. And to add to the levels of meaning, surely all this discussion has links with the problem of involvement which I spoke of in the first chapter, just as it is connected with the important theme which I shall discuss in the next chapter, that of relationships, not only those between the individual characters, but also between narrator and reader, and their complementary roles in the elucidation of truth.

I have spent some time discussing this one passage, which began with a reference to the potential power of the author as an inventor, or conveyer, of stories. This is of course only one of many points at which the narrator contrasts the endless possibilities open to the imagination with his own alleged commitment to the truth. Such remarks are especially frequent in the earlier part of *Jacques*, but crop up from time to time throughout it, and there is an interesting one near the end (pp.278-79). Here the narrator runs through the various possibilities open to him, or which would be open to him if he were 'un faiseur de roman'. But 'mon projet est d'être vrai', he says, 'je l'ai rempli'. Then he appears to contradict himself by saying that since the reader has no evidence that the abbé Hudson is dead, 'il est donc mort ou vivant comme il me plaira'. There follows another range of possibilities, introduced, as so often, by 'il ne tiendrait qu'à moi de [...]' and then the by now predictable assurance that such things are the province of the novelist; whereas our narrator will stick to the truth.

By now, any moderately alert reader must have wondered why Diderot is so insistent on this point. Huguette Cohen allots a special section to it (*16*, pp.109-13) which deals both with the different forms it takes and the reactions of various critics to it. The main point I want to make here is that Diderot must not be taken too literally. It is obvious of course that he is not exploiting all the resources of the novelist, but it is equally obvious that he is not telling the truth in the usual sense of the word. Apart from the fact that the whole of *Jacques*, with the exception of a few intercalated stories and references, is

fictional, Diderot does quite often resort to the traditional
devices of popular fiction. There is a minor adventure early on
in the story, when Jacques and his master find themselves in an
inn full of brigands (pp.41-43); and another near the end (p.325)
when Jacques's master kills Saint-Ouin, and Jacques is marched
off to prison. There are unlikely coincidences, like the arrival of
the funeral hearse (p.82), which seems to be carrying Jacques's
captain's body to the grave; or the fact that Saint-Ouin should
have chosen just that day to go and visit Agathe's child and thus
meet his death from Jacques's master's sword. The difference
between these events and the similar ones which appear in
traditional novels is that Diderot makes no pretence of
integrating them into the story: nothing leads us to expect them,
and they have no apparent consequences. (I say 'apparent'
because I shall have something more to say about this in the
chapter on Destiny). Like so much else in *Jacques*, these
incidents are a parody of what happens in a 'real' novel. The
effect of Diderot's repeated claim that he is giving us the truth is
not to reassure us, not to present us with an answer, but with a
question: 'What is truth?' or better, perhaps, 'What are you
really expecting when you ask for the truth?'

Diderot is parodying the reader's double expectation, fostered
by the average novelist, of hearing something which is both
interesting and carries a guarantee of truth. When he rejects the
kind of development which 'aurait pué le *Cleveland* à infecter' in
favour of the truth (p.71), he allows the reader to make an
objection: 'La vérité, me direz-vous, est souvent froide,
commune et plate', like the account of Jacques being bandaged.
Here, then, the reader is not asking for truth at all; he is asking
to be entertained. At other times Diderot parodies the demand
for factual truth. The story of Jacques's captain and his friend,
he says, is not a 'conte' (p.99); he, the narrator, has heard it
himself 'aux Invalides, je ne sais en quelle année, le jour de
Saint-Louis, à table chez un monsieur de Saint-Etienne, major
de l'hôtel'. The details are convincing, and the fact that he has
forgotten which year it was makes it somehow more convincing,
and he goes on to give an oblique telling-off to anyone who
thought it was invented.

But is it invented or not? We do not know, and besides, it does not much matter, at least in any one particular case. What we do know is that some of Diderot's anecdotes, such as the one about Prémontval (p.101), or the Hudson story (p.220 and note 3), concern real people, while some do not, and that there is no evidence within the text, beyond the narrator's deliberately unreliable statements, as to their truth. This is another indication by Diderot that truth of this kind is not what he, or we, are concerned with. To emphasize the point he sometimes offers absurd examples of doubtful evidence, as though he were the meticulous editor of an imperfect manuscript. When Jacques has finally drunk up the champagne after the story of Madame de La Pommeraye, the narrator tells us there are two versions of what he did next (pp.200-01): one that he stretched out on some chairs, the other that he ended up on the floor, and then, to make his point clear, he tells us to choose between them. As usual, we are in the realms of parody.

At other times, the narrator is not uncertain which version to choose, he has simply forgotten, and in one case, having offered us a number of possible places for Jacques and his master to spend the night (pp.57-58), he remembers later on where it was (p.62). The best-known choice of versions is of course offered to us in the final pages of the book, when three possible endings are given for Jacques's story, all presented as highly suspect, and one openly based on *Tristram Shandy*. What Diderot knows will happen is that we shall not try to decide between the three versions but will simply read each of them with the pleasure it deserves. It would seem then that the truth, in the case of *Jacques le fataliste*, is not to be taken as one of the possible versions with which the narrator presents us, nor in fact anything which we can see on the printed page, but the truth we can learn about ourselves, and the true nature of the demands we make on the novelist and story-teller in general.

One of the chief purposes of Diderot's constant interruptions (and I have not by any means dealt with all of his devices for breaking the flow of the narrative) is to remind us that we are listening to a story. He delights in taking the story away from us, so to speak, in order to remind us how artificial the situation is.

If we respond to the challenge we ask ourselves why we object —
as we surely do — and go on to wonder what it really is that we
are looking for when we listen to a story. To try to give a clear-
cut answer to that question would be to do violence to Diderot's
intentions. All this book can do, and perhaps should do, is to
provide a number of pointers. As I shall try to show in the next
chapter, *Jacques* is very much concerned with relationships. One
of these relationships is between ourselves and the text, and what
the book has to offer is contained in the relationship we set up
with it, and the way we respond to the challenges it constantly
makes.

In any case, Diderot also implies that the literal truth is
impossible to convey. 'Dis la chose comme elle est', says
Jacques's master (p.89), whereupon Jacques lists the various
factors which make this impossible, and which can be summed
up as the differing individual characteristics of teller and
listener, 'd'où il doit arriver que deux fois à peine en un jour,
dans toute une grande ville, on soit entendu comme on dit'. And
this uncertainty applies not only to assessments of fact but to
moral judgements: 'on n'y fait presque rien qui soit jugé comme
on l'a fait' (p.90). This is a central theme of *Jacques*, and
particularly of the separate stories it contains, but the point
which is relevant to this chapter is the implication that the novels
we read are not in fact grounded in truth, but on a convention.
They are not only fiction in the ordinary sense, that is, invented
stories, they are based on the fiction that a story can be
understood in the same terms as it is told. Diderot goes to great
pains to show us that this is impossible, and that truth in books,
or rather the truth we get *from* books, as from life, is the
product of a two-way process set up between giver and receiver.

The conventional nature of the average novel is also dealt with
on a more technical level. When Jacques has to go back to
collect the purse and his master's watch (pp.58-60), the narrator
confesses to a dilemma: he does not know whether to go with
Jacques or stay with Jacques's master. At first sight the problem
seems absurd, another piece of teasing on the part of Diderot, as
though the narrator were actually there all the time with his
characters. But it does reveal one of the fictions on which novels

are based, that the narrator, and consequently his reader, are not subject to the spatial and temporal limitations imposed on real human beings. In other words we are not usually worried about a story-teller being in two places at once. Now one might say that this is still not a problem. Why should the narrator not have heard accounts of the two men's activities from separate sources, perhaps even from their own lips, and included them both in his account? This would not be stretching the claim to veracity too far.

I think that this is one of the points where it is helpful to take account of a peculiarly eighteenth-century way of looking at the problem. Among the sources of the novel, it will be recalled, were the personal memoirs of the seventeenth century and these memoirs were usually put forward as eye-witness accounts of political and military events as experienced by someone involved in them. As such they claimed to provide a guarantee of truth, in opposition to the official, authoritative histories, which presented a global and politically slanted view of things. This was part of an attitude which became much more general in the eighteenth century, the conviction that personal experience was the only valid substitute for the increasingly discredited authority of Church and State. It was an attitude which affected all areas of thinking, and the novel had, at least in theory, responded to this desire for accounts based on personal experience (and usually narrated in the first person). For this reason, the concept of the eye-witness, the person who experiences things at first hand, has a privileged status in eighteenth-century thought as a foundation for truth. Any narrator who pretends to a more complete view of things than an eye-witness might provide is therefore giving us something more than our direct experience of life can provide. The truth he offers is not the same as truth to life as we live it, and he could be said to be assuming an authority to which he has no right.

Not that there is necessarily anything wrong in this: Diderot is simply helping us to understand what we want from a novelist. Indeed the fault, if there is one, lies as much with the reader as the narrator, for, to return to the example from *Jacques*, we are really interested in knowing what happens to both men, and it is only when Jacques's master turns out to be boring that we want to stay with Jacques. 'Eh bien! en avez-vous assez du maître, et son valet ne venant point à nous, voulez-vous que nous allions à lui?' (p.60).

There are variations on this theme throughout the book. At the very beginning (p.35) we are reminded that the usual details we demand about characters in a story are not necessarily provided by an eye-witness, or by our experience of life. The incident of the menacing peasants (pp.46-47), to which I shall return, is an example of an eye-witness incident, but, as it happens, one which has nothing to do with Jacques and his master, and it acts as a reminder that we ask our authors to exercise a certain amount of selection. We are not interested in the irrelevancies which regularly crop up in real life. When Jacques's horse carries him off (pp.98-99), the narrator, having reminded us that Jacques and his master are only interesting when they are together, suggests that he have a chat with us until Jacques's return. The assumption made here that narrative time is simultaneous with present time, that the eye-witness must amuse himself until something happens again, is rather different, of course, but still serves to remind us of the gap between our own reality and that of a story. Another variation is the narrator's sudden involvement in the story (p.123): 'Là, j'entends un vacarme [...]', which leads the reader to intervene: 'Vous entendez! Vous n'y étiez pas', and points up from another angle the absurdity of the eye-witness fiction. Once again, the possibility of a dependable criterion of truth is removed.

I have said that the truth, or at least *a* truth offered by *Jacques* concerns the demands we make on the novelist. This has led a number of critics in recent years to see *Jacques* primarily as a book about the novel in general and the problems associated with it. 'S'il y a enquête dans *Jacques le fataliste*, c'est donc enquête sur le roman' (*1*, p.cxxiii), say Lecointre and Le Galliot in their introduction. This is an interesting and fruitful approach, all the more so because much modern literary criticism, and many modern novels, are concerned with literature as a kind of examination of itself, as a self-contained, self-conscious world which relates only to itself. *Jacques le fataliste* would thus be an early, and rare, example of a preoccupation which has become more general in our own age. Certainly Diderot does use *Jacques* as a means of reflecting on the nature of the novel, and it is true that he uses parody and other techniques to reflect upon ways in which the novel tries to give the appearance of life, but this need not necessarily mean that the problem of the novel is the endpoint of the discussion.

In an incident which I have already mentioned in another context, involving the brigands at the inn (pp.41-43), there is a point where Jacques walks into their room with a pistol in each hand and tells them to go to bed, threatening to blow out the brains of the first one who makes a false move. 'Jacques avait l'air et le ton si vrais', the narrative continues, 'que ces coquins, qui prisaient autant la vie que d'honnêtes gens, se lèvent de table sans souffler un mot, se déshabillent et se couchent.' Jacques has acted in so convincing, or, one might say, so lifelike a way, that the brigands are taken in and do as he says. This is one of those occasions when we are encouraged to apply to a 'real' event the criteria which we normally use for art. Jacques's behaviour had such a strong semblance of truth, was so 'vraisemblable', that he was believed. When he returns, his master asks what would have happened if the brigands had refused to cooperate, but Jacques claims that this is impossible 'parce qu'ils ne l'ont pas fait'. The answer seems absurd, unless, of course, we are talking about a story, in which case there is some sense in it.

Diderot has blurred the distinction between life and the novel, or fact and fiction, in two ways. He has implied firstly that effective action in life can be judged by the same standards as effective art (a point he develops in *Le Paradoxe sur le comédien*); and secondly that Jacques has the fatalistic attitude to life which we would judge entirely appropriate to a fictional character, whose fate is already written. I shall take up this point in the chapter on Destiny.

Diderot introduces a further variation on the theme of 'vraisemblance' a few pages later (pp.46-47) when, having escaped from the inn, Jacques and his master hear a noise behind them and turn round to see a menacing crowd rushing towards them with goads and pitchforks. 'Vous allez croire', the narrator says, and tells us, no doubt correctly, who we shall think they are, and what they are doing. The troop of men have unwittingly put on a convincing performance, giving the impression to Jacques and ourselves of being a party from the inn, bent on retribution. They too had 'l'air et le ton si vrais' that they imposed a temporary semblance of reality, but one which this time turned out to be false.

Jacques has then, in this sequence of events, succeeded on one occasion in imposing his own version of things on the brigands, and on another has been taken in by the world around him. If we look at the novel as a whole, we find that this is one of its recurrent themes. People are constantly trying to impose their version of reality on others, or else are the victims of other people's versions of reality. On the whole, Jacques comes out fairly well in these contests. The stories of his early love-life, with Justine (pp.239-48), Suzanne and Marguerite (pp.250-56) are stories of minor confidence tricks played on more or less willing victims; he is successful with the brigands, and also in retrieving his master's watch (pp.60-64), but on the other hand he has to pay for a night with a girl he has never seen (pp.64-65); and at the end of the story things go badly wrong when he is taken to prison for his master's crime (p.325). His master tends to be a victim, sometimes of Jacques's version of things, and consistently of his friend's, Saint-Ouin (pp.266-76; 279-96; 311-15). The two most important tales, those of Madame de La Pommeraye and Hudson, are also stories of confidence tricks.

In each case we can ask the question — and I think we are encouraged to ask it by Diderot — is there any essential difference between Jacques, Saint-Ouin, Madame de La Pommeraye, Hudson and the others on the one hand, and a story-teller or novelist on the other? The only character who claims not to be trying to tell a convincing story is the narrator, who consistently denies us the involvement in his stories which would both give us pleasure and allow us to be taken in. He refuses to play the game, and thus helps us to see how the game is played. By his constant interruptions, by introducing the unexpected, by raising questions about truth and fiction, the nature of evidence, the status of truth, and so on, he forces us to think. And the thoughts we are encouraged to have are surely not just about the nature of the novel, but about the nature of life as we experience it from moment to moment.

Another recurrent, and associated, theme suggests that we all have something of the story-teller in us. We are reminded, if we needed reminding, of Jacques's love of talking, when the narrator pauses to tell us about people's motives for going to see executions (pp.216-17). 'Il va chercher en Grève une scène qu'il puisse raconter à son retour dans le faubourg; cella-là ou une autre, cela lui est indifférent, pourvu qu'il s'en fasse écouter.' The story, as we tell it, makes us a person of consequence, and Jacques is only one of many compulsive narrators in the story. We come across a brief example quite early on (pp.37-38) in the surgeon who insists on explaining about the structure of the knee-joint: 'je veux leur démontrer, et je leur démontrerai ...' Later on (p.90) we have 'l'orateur du coin, qui ne demandait pas mieux que de pérorer', and these are followed by a stream of episodic characters who expound, explain, and above all, tell stories. Perhaps the greatest talker of them all, apart from Jacques, is the hostess at the inn, who tells the story of Madame de La Pommeraye; 'sa passion dominante [...] c'était celle de parler' (p.143).

Here is a theme which again opens out onto life and human nature. Story-telling, and by implication story-writing, are seen not as specialized activities, but as an aspect of the need to push oneself forward, to be at the centre of things, and to impose one's view of things on others. Significantly, the passage just quoted on this subject (pp.216-17) follows an observation by Jacques about the need felt by even the poorest people to keep a dog (p.214). 'D'où il conclut que tout homme voulait commander à un autre; et que l'animal se trouvant dans la société immédiatement au-dessous de la classe des derniers citoyens commandés par toutes les autres classes, ils prenaient un animal pour commander aussi à quelqu'un.' Jacques's view of society is that everyone is someone else's dog, and that real dogs are the slaves of those who are too low in the social scale to find anyone else to order about. The implication is that we all want power over others, and the specific link with the broader subject of *Jacques* is made on the two pages which, after a brief interruption, follow. A temporary feeling of power can come from talking, from having something to relate which someone else wants to hear. It is this power which the narrator delights in reminding us of throughout the novel, and here a new element is introduced. The narrator not only has things to tell us, he can also make them up, and this implies not just the exercise of power, but the possibility of its abuse.

This discussion might seem to have drifted a long way from the subject of this chapter, truth and fiction, but this is in a sense right, because Diderot himself in *Jacques le fataliste* wants to direct us away from our rather literal interpretation of truth, and its opposition to fiction. He does not exactly deny that such a distinction exists, he is telling us that it is not what matters. The content of a novel is in reality based on an unspoken convention made between author and reader, an uneasy marriage of truth, or the appearance of truth, and entertainment. Because there are no clear rules attached to this convention, it is open to abuse, and thus presents a parallel with our conduct of life, which is an uneasy relationship between ourselves and others, or between ourselves and the things that happen to us.

3. Relationships

It is probably not an exaggeration to say that the whole structure of *Jacques le fataliste* is based on relationships. The pattern is set as soon as the book begins. Instead of a story, introduced in the traditional way as though it were an objective account of a series of events, we have a somewhat petulant outburst by a narrator who is already impatient with his reader's questions. Moreover, the book actually starts with a reader's question: we, or rather the figure set up to represent us, are making our narrative requirements felt from the very beginning, and the narrator feels the need to put us in our place. One could describe the whole of *Jacques* as an attempt to define that place, given the fact that as the narrative proceeds we become concerned with much more than the demands we should make of a story-teller.

I have referred in the course of the preceding chapters to many of the features which define the developing relationships between narrator and reader, but before going any further it is as well to emphasize that we cannot identify the reader with ourselves, any more than the narrator is identical with Diderot. Even if all the questions asked by the reader were to coincide exactly with those we wished to ask ourselves (and very often they probably do), the whole point of this device is to place us at one remove from this dialogue and to make us reflect about the implications of the narrator/reader relationship. And it is important to remember, as we read, that the traditional function of the author in a novel of this period was either to efface himself completely, in order to give the illusion that his story is a self-contained world, with its own objective status, or else to intervene in order to guarantee the authenticity of the events and characters he is describing.

The narrator in *Jacques* declines to subscribe to this convention. He refuses to play the game. The various ways in which he does not play the game are usefully tabulated by Eric

Walter (*19*, pp.29-30). If it is possible to select one passage
which typifies the general approach, it is perhaps the point
where the reader is assumed to be fed up with the story of
Gousse and wants to go back to Jacques and his master (p.103).
'Je vous entends; vous en avez assez, et votre avis serait que nous
allassions rejoindre nos deux voyageurs. Lecteur, vous me
traitez comme un automate, cela n'est pas poli.' The narrator
objects to being treated like a mechanical toy, as though his role
is simply to perform for the reader's amusement. He is insisting
on his rights as an equal partner: 'Il faut sans doute que j'aille
quelquefois à votre fantaisie; mais il faut que j'aille quelquefois
à la mienne'. We might ask of course what right the narrator has
to these grand ideas. After all, we are the consumers, and we
should get what we want. But what *do* we want? This is the
question we are encouraged to ask ourselves throughout the
book, and the general answer seems to be that we claim to want
the truth (whatever that might be), but that in fact we have
other, conflicting requirements: to know more than we could
reasonably discover in real life (as in the opening lines), to be
constantly entertained (the Pondicherry story), not to be
shocked (the commentary on Jacques's early love-life, pp.260-
62), and so on.

We are thus accused of making unreasonable demands, and
the answer we are offered is not that we should be more careful
about what we want, but that we should lower our expectations
and adopt a policy of give-and-take: 'votre fantaisie [...] la
mienne'. And not only do we regularly get reminded of this
duty, we are also allowed to intervene ourselves to keep the
narrator within bounds: 'On entend un vacarme effroyable. Je
vois deux hommes [...] — Vous ne voyez rien; il ne s'agit pas de
vous, vous n'y étiez pas — Il est vrai [...]' (p.123). Sometimes
the narrator spontaneously admits his own transgressions:
'Lecteur, il me vient un scrupule, c'est d'avoir fait honneur à
Jacques ou à son maître de quelques réflexions qui vous
appartiennent de droit; si cela est, vous pouvez les reprendre
sans qu'ils s'en formalisent' (p.249), or confesses that words like
'engastrimute' (p.264), or 'hydrophobe' (p.310) were preferences of his own, and not authentic utterances of Jacques.

Diderot thus leads us away from any attempt to determine exactly what the proper subject-matter of a novel should be and leads us into another area entirely, that of mutual respect between narrator and reader. Needless to say, the subject is not exhausted in the exchanges between these two figures. As we should expect from the structure of *Jacques*, the theme is taken up in other ways. I have already drawn attention in the previous chapter to the explicit comparison made between Jacques's master and the reader. To continue the quotation after 'homme questionneur comme vous, lecteur [...]', it goes on '— Et pourquoi questionnait-il? — Belle question! Il questionnait pour apprendre et pour redire comme vous, lecteur [...]' (pp.83-84); and this last point should remind us of the observations made about people who go to see executions so that they can come back and tell their friends all about it (pp.216-17). Jacques's master is therefore linked with ourselves on the one hand and with human nature in general on the other, and his exchanges with Jacques must be interpreted with this in mind.

The comparison is not of course very flattering. 'Il a peu d'idées dans la tête; s'il lui arrive de dire quelque chose de sensé, c'est de réminiscence ou d'inspiration. Il a des yeux comme vous et moi; mais on ne sait la plupart du temps s'il regarde. Il ne dort pas, il ne veille pas non plus; il se laisse exister: c'est sa fonction habituelle' (p.59). This description is important. With what follows, it is the fullest attempt Diderot makes to characterize him, and, at first sight, he turns out to be something of a freak. He is also called an 'automate', and, as we are told, something quite new to us: 'vous ne connaissez pas encore cette espèce-là'. These details, together with the watch and the snuff-box, more or less complete the description of Jacques's master, at least for the time being. Why should Diderot have invented such a strange and limited character for such an important role? The answer probably lies in the parallel with the reader which I have just mentioned. He is, essentially, a 'lecteur', ourselves in our role as readers, materialized in parodic form in the text. As a reader, or more properly a listener, he has no existence beyond his relationship with Jacques, without whom he is lost. Anything interesting he has to say comes from his past, or from somewhere outside him, 'de réminiscence ou d'inspiration'; 'il se laisse exister', because he depends, as a listener, on the stimulus provided by Jacques. Finally, the remark 'vous ne connaissez pas encore cette espèce-là' is surely a piece of irony, or teasing, on Diderot's part.

Nevertheless, the master is not quite as vegetable-like as Diderot's description might suggest. Apart from his role as a listener, he also has a number of opinions ('de réminiscence', presumably), and a certain uneasiness about his relationship with Jacques, which manifests itself from time to time in explosions of anger. These three aspects of his personality together define his relationship with Jacques, which in turn provides a caricature, a commentary and a new perspective on the narrator/reader relationship which I discussed earlier.

Firstly, as a listener to Jacques, the master can show in an exaggerated, caricatured form the aberrations to which we are all subject. Sometimes he is detached, making humorous comments on Jacques's situation: 'Te voilà en chirurgiens comme Saint-Roch en chapeaux ' (p.48). At others he becomes involved. He condemns Jacques when he sees what he is about to do to Justine (p.244): 'Traître! scélérat! sais-tu quel crime tu vas commettrè? Tu vas violer cette fille [...]', and his cries of 'scélérat' punctuate the further developments in Jacques's story of his early loves. This is a rather exaggerated case of moral disapproval — or could it be ribald complicity? — in respect of what happened many years before, and it is accompanied by the illusion on his part that he is actually there. A better example (already alluded to) of this kind of involvement is his reaction to Jacques's account of being attacked by bandits after his act of generosity to the girl who broke her pitcher of oil (p.118). 'Mon maître, qu'avez-vous? Vous serrez les dents, vous vous agitez comme si vous étiez en présence d'un ennemi', says Jacques, interrupting his story, and his master agrees: 'J'y suis, en effet; j'ai l'épée à la main; je fonds sur tes voleurs et je te venge'. A little later he throws his arms round Jacques, unable to see how he can escape his predicament, so that Jacques has to reassure him: 'Mon maître, rassurez-vous, me voilà'. Of course, Jacques's master's moments of involvement are much more extreme than anything the average reader is likely to experience, but their exaggerated form points up more clearly what the mechanism of involvement is. This applies especially to the loss of a sense of time, when narrative time and present time are merged into one.

Like the reader too, the master plays an active critical role in the story-telling process, interrupting Jacques, giving his own views, making his preferences plain, and so on. And here too, the fact that he is a character in the plot (for want of a vaguer word), and not, as in the case of the 'lecteur', a figure who is outside the action, makes it easier to define his role. The general pattern is defined, as in the case of the 'lecteur', by his desire to hear the story of Jacques's love-life, but unlike his role in life, his role as a listener is by no means passive. Apart from the tendency already mentioned to lose himself in the story, he allows himself to be distracted into discussions, requests for details and other stories. In the course of Jacques's stories, it becomes clear that the relationship is very much a two-way one, as for example when Jacques suddenly realizes that his master has stopped listening to him (p.87). It turns out that he wants an explanation for a mysterious comment made by one of the followers of the captain's hearse, and Jacques is forced to break off his own story and provide the explanation, since, as his master points out, 'quand tu parleras, tu veux apparemment être écouté?' But Jacques makes a condition of his own, that his master will not interrupt. As of course is to be expected, the history of Jacques's captain is not allowed to proceed without interruption, either by the master or by outside events, but at least a standard is set: mutual consideration, give and take, is established as the aim in their relationship.

Later on we find further developments of this theme. When Jacques's master is relating his own story about Saint-Ouin, Jacques interrupts him (p.284), to make some observations, one of which is on the subject of interruptions: 'je n'ai jamais pu suivre mon histoire sans qu'un diable ou un autre m'interrompît, et [...] la vôtre va tout de suite. Voilà le train de la vie [...]'; at which he is criticized by his master for complaining about being interrupted and then interrupting

himself (p.285). Even when Jacques, by a soft answer, avoids
the dispute which threatens to erupt, his master takes him to task
again, this time for taking away the story-teller's pleasure: 'Tu
vas anticipant sur le raconteur, et tu lui ôtes le plaisir qu'il s'est
promis de ta surprise; en sorte qu'ayant, par une ostentation de
sagacité très déplacée, deviné ce qu'il avait à te dire, il ne lui reste
plus qu'à se taire, et je me tais' (p.285).

Both criticisms express the master's claim to what one might
call 'story-teller's rights', but however much a narrator may feel
he has a right to tell his story to the end without interruption,
this hardly ever happens in *Jacques le fataliste*, and, Diderot
implies, hardly ever in life either. This is borne out by the well-
known opening lines of one of Diderot's short stories, *Ceci n'est
pas un conte*: 'Lorsqu'on fait un conte, c'est à quelqu'un qui
l'écoute; et pour peu que le conte dure, il est rare que le conteur
ne soit pas interrompu quelquefois par son auditeur' (*3*, p.821).

What then is Diderot trying to tell us through his frequent
examples of the shifting relationship between teller and listener,
whether it be the 'narrateur' and 'lecteur', or Jacques and his
master, or, one supposes, Diderot and ourselves? He certainly
cannot be saying that we should, as Jacques's master seems to
want, always listen in silence to a story-teller. Nor for that
matter is he telling us that there is any set of clear-cut rules,
which, if followed, would enable all narrators and listeners to
narrate and listen happily ever after. It would be a mistake —
indeed it is nearly always a mistake where literature is concerned
— to think that the writer is proposing a set of guidelines for
behaviour which can be worked out from a study of the text.
Few works of literature are as obviously didactic as this, and
although, as I shall try to show in the final chapter, *Jacques le
fataliste* may be more didactic than most, its message, or lesson,
is not being communicated at this rather straightforward level.
In any case, one could hardly imagine that Diderot would write a
work of this length and complexity just to lay down some guidelines about the relation and reception of stories.

As I suggested in the previous chapter, the narrator/reader
element is part of a much larger theme which is illustrated by
Jacques and his master, for they have a relationship which goes

far beyond that of narrator and listener: they are also master and servant. This element, although it might not at first sight seem relevant to the parallel with the reader/narrator aspect, has in fact often been compared with it. It is connected with the theme of power, but enables it to be viewed from a different angle from the one I mentioned in the last chapter (of story-telling as a means of acquiring temporary power over others). In the case of Jacques and his master, the distribution of power is apparently built in to the relationship. This is evident not only from the fact that Jacques works as his master's servant, but also at the level of story-telling, where the master claims the right to 'interrompre son valet, l'interrompre tant qu'il lui plaît, et n'en pas être interrompu' (p.285), but as we are regularly reminded in the course of the dialogue, this relationship is rarely observed, either at this level or at any other. Immediately after this statement by the master, the narrator recalls another dispute between master and servant, the one which was finally settled by the hostess at the inn, and which contains the fullest treatment of the problem (pp.207-13).

This argument begins with Jacques's refusal to accept his master's view of his subordinate status, since, as he rightly claims, he is a more capable and necessary person. When the argument between them threatens to become violent, the hostess intervenes and delivers her parody of a judicial pronouncement. What it amounts to is that, once this dispute is out of the way, the question shall never be raised again, the question, that is, of who is master; 'et qu'il soit laissé, entre ce que l'un peut et ce que l'autre doit, la même obscurité que ci-devant' (p.210). The implication of this final comment is that formal relationships such as that between Jacques and his master have no necessary connection with the reality of things. A master is officially the dominant figure, but there is no reason why he should be the stronger personality; moreover, whether stronger or not, he cannot do without his servant: each exists by virtue of the other. The further reference to a political dispute (p.210, and the explanatory note) suggests that the same is true of the sovereign and his people. The real distribution of power between them does not correspond to the official fiction that the sovereign is

master and the people are his subjects, so that, here too, it is
safer if the dangerous reality is not talked about, if the official
fiction is respected.

But this is not the end of the story, for Jacques's master now
succumbs to a fit of emotion in which he admits his own
inferiority to Jacques. Then Jacques, who is not content with the
situation as it stands, makes his stipulations, which amount to
the fact firstly, that he will remain free to do as he likes,
secondly, that 'qu'attendu qu'il est aussi impossible à Jacques de
ne pas connaître son ascendant et sa force sur son maître, qu'à
son maître de méconnaître sa faiblesse et de se dépouiller de son
indulgence, il faut que Jacques soit insolent, et que, pour la
paix, son maître ne s'en aperçoive pas' (pp.211-12). This is
perhaps the most important passage in this section. It gives
formal recognition to what has already happened: Jacques's
master has been unable not to admit his subordinate role, and
Jacques has felt obliged to assert his dominance. Each has
respected the letter of the hostess's judgement, but not its spirit.
Now Jacques's own stipulation defines the reality of the
relationship, which always has been, and will continue to be,
conditioned by their respective characters; but at the same time,
'pour la paix', his master will pretend not to notice Jacques's
abuses of his official position as servant.

All this might seem to be an unsatisfactory solution, and
indeed the relations between Jacques and his master continue to
be unsatisfactory, especially towards the end of the story, when
the master, having killed Saint-Ouin, runs away and leaves
Jacques to take the consequences (p.325). But — and this is
surely Diderot's point — what sort of arrangement can be
satisfactory when life so regularly fails to fit in with the order we
should like to impose on it? We have our formal relationships:
king and subjects, master and servant, narrator and listener, and
so on, but we can never be sure how far the people involved will
be willing, or able, to perform these roles. So the best we can do
is, as Jacques suggests, to remember what the formal situation is
at the same time as we make the best we can of the reality.

The dispute I have just discussed is not explicitly concerned
with the narrator/listener relationship with which I began, and is

another indication that Diderot wants to go beyond the problems of story-telling to talk about attitudes to other people in general. In fact there are a number of other relationships which act as commentaries on this theme. Some of them are contained in the (more or less) separate stories, and these I shall discuss in the next chapter; but in addition we have, among others, the case of Jacques's captain and his duelling partner, and that of the kindly executioner. The case of the duelling partners comes in two parts, the description of the actual relationship (pp.94-98) and the narrator's reflections on it (pp.103-05). A story of two men who are drawn together by an irresistible attraction and yet are constantly trying to kill each other represents the ultimate absurdity in human relationships, and the whole narrative is made more absurd by the fact that Jacques is interrupted at irregular intervals by his horse's refusal to keep its head straight.

The later reflections put the situation in a different light. Here is a much more serious, and finally rather moving passage, in which, after various motives are considered for this strange behaviour, the problem is then seen as a survival from the past and finally as simply a way of testing one's own superiority, an activity which appears in society 'sous toutes sortes de formes, entre des prêtres, entre des magistrats, entre des littérateurs, entre des philosophes' (p.104). The problem is not solved: perhaps the captain and his duelling partner belong to one of these categories, perhaps to all of them. But what might have seemed at first to be an exceptional circumstance is finally presented as just one example of typical human behaviour, and connected, as so often in *Jacques le fataliste*, with our need to feel power over others.

The case of the executioner, which immediately follows (pp.105-09), again deals with an exceptional circumstance, this time of a man whose profession makes him universally disliked and avoided (at least in the eighteenth century), but who nevertheless puts himself out to help Jacques when he is knocked unconscious. More important than the incident itself however is Jacques's reaction to it. Unaware of the man's profession, he is overcome with gratitude and respect for him, the more so because the executioner reacts coldly to him, behaviour which indicates to Jacques that he has 'une longue habitude de bienfaisance' (p.108). The executioner has failed to come up (or down) to his formal role in society. Character and function, as so often, refuse to fit, and Jacques misjudges the situation. The incident itself has no further influence on the story, but it adds to the cumulative effect of all the unpredictable and intractable people and events regarding which Jacques, or his master, or we ourselves, are sometimes correct in our assessments and sometimes completely taken in.

A point worth noting is that, in this area of judgements, Diderot makes very little difference between people and events. Jacques's misjudgement of the executioner's role in life is on a par with the appearance of the menacing peasants, who turn out not to present the threat he had feared (p.46) or the passing of the funeral cortège which may or may not be that of his captain (pp.82-83; 88). In life, as in a story, or a novel, our judgement of both people and events (and usually it is a combination of the two) is based on the incomplete evidence available and on our experience, and there is no way of predicting whether they will lead us to the right answer or not. Nevertheless we cannot help ourselves from acting as though we can know what is happening. We are not necessarily reduced to a state of resigned inactivity by our continued failure to understand and control what happens around us. We do not, in other words, become fatalists, in the popularly accepted sense of the word. When they tell their stories, both Jacques and his master object to the other's trying to guess what is coming; the narrator objects to the reader wanting extra information. But there is never any suggestion that listeners and readers will therefore stop asking for information to which, as it were, they have no right, any more than one stops asking life for the certainty it cannot provide.

At this level the themes I have been discussing can be brought together. The contest between narrator and reader, between master and servant, between various individuals, and between the individual and his experience of life are all part of a power struggle in which each tries to gain the dominant position. Unlike the power struggles which we see in some of the episodic stories, and in most novels, the relationship between narrator and reader, and between Jacques and his master, contain a kind of commentary upon themselves. We are, if we remain alert, reminded of what is really going on when we read or listen to a story, or when we involve ourselves with another person. *Jacques le fataliste* does not however try to correct our behaviour: it accepts that we shall carry on behaving like this. This is one aspect of its originality: by suggesting that our attitudes to other people mirror our attitudes to life, and to stories about life, it puts forward the view that all consist in two-way relationships, paradoxical ones, in that although there is not much we can do about them, we still have a responsibility for what they are.

4. Stories and Anecdotes

The two stories which stand out from the rest in *Jacques le fataliste*, both by their length and seriousness, are those of Madame de La Pommeraye (pp.144-50; 161-95) and the abbé Hudson (pp.220-32). Apart from these the novel is punctuated by a series of stories, anecdotes and fables ranging from several pages to a paragraph. All of these are recounted either by Jacques, or his master, or the narrator, and this is another feature which distinguishes them from the first two, which are told respectively by the hostess at the inn and the Marquis des Arcis. What they all have in common is that they deal with cases of unusual behaviour. Sometimes this behaviour is simply exaggerated or obsessive, as in the case of the poet of Pondicherry, who cannot stop writing poetry, or the philanthropic Le Pelletier, who cannot stop giving to the poor; but in most of the stories, some kind of moral problem is also raised. For this reason the stories are always included in critical discussions of the moral import of *Jacques*.

The other aspect of *Jacques* to which they are generally regarded as relevant is its structure. A quite thorough discussion of the most important views on this problem can be found in Chapter II, 'A la recherche d'une structure' of Cohen (*16*, pp.55-83). The more successful attempts to see how the stories fit into the structure have been those which link them most closely to the subject-matter. One of the best features of Laufer's article (*11*) is that it shows how subject-matter and structure go hand in hand, each supporting and illuminating the other. For this reason I shall discuss the two aspects together in this chapter. I have in any case indicated that it is unwise, with *Jacques le fataliste*, to separate out the various elements beyond what is absolutely necessary for discussion purposes. As Cohen says (*16*, p.82), 'Tout effort de décomposition du roman, qui le démonte et le recompose comme un puzzle, risque de trahir les intentions de Diderot'.

To return to the longer of the two main stories, that of Madame de La Pommeraye is clearly intended to occupy a key position in the novel. It takes quite a long time to get started, but eventually builds up a momentum which carries it along with apparent inevitability to its surprise ending. The fact that the latter part of it is recounted late at night enables it to proceed without the interruptions which punctuate the hostess's life during her working day, and this is surely intended by Diderot so that, in contrast with the frequent distractions of the earlier part, we are, here at least, given a story in which we, like Jacques and his master, can really get involved. This story is something of a set piece, in which Diderot uses all his skill as a story-teller to prepare as convincingly as possible the grotesque disaster which is to befall the Marquis des Arcis. It is the only story which could reasonably be isolated from the novel and read for its own sake.

Its main interest lies in the extraordinary, single-minded plan of Madame de La Pommeraye to take her revenge on des Arcis for falling out of love with her, but one could say that the root of the problem lies in her original expectation that their liaison should be permanent. She has demanded constancy from a world whose nature it is to be inconstant. This is confirmed by the 'poetic' passage which introduces the discussion of love by Jacques and his master after the first part of the story (p.151), and by the fable of 'La Gaine et le Coutelet' which follows it (p.152). The fable makes the point (not exactly a moral one, as Jacques's master says) that it is not changing partners which is wrong, but promising not to change in the first place. Both des Arcis and Madame de La Pommeraye have been unwise, then, in making a promise which could not be kept. This is going against the nature of things, and it is also going against the spirit of *Jacques le fataliste*, which recognizes the inconstancy of story-tellers and listeners to a story once begun, or the impossibility of someone like Jacques remaining firm in his obligation to obey his master. This latter point, significantly, is dealt with in the incident which immediately follows the Pommeraye story.

But Madame de La Pommeraye refuses to accept this view of

life. Instead of accepting her fate with resignation she decides to bend the Marquis to her will. If we are talking about struggles for power, which is one of the themes of *Jacques*, then we can say that her struggle is not so much with des Arcis himself as with life, or fate. And if we consider it in the light of the story-telling theme, we can say that she writes her own story with flesh-and-blood characters. She takes Madame and Mademoiselle d'Aisnon, divests them of their earlier occupation as prostitutes, and recreates them, with new characters and a new way of life (pp.165-66), for the fulfilment of her project. What she demands above all is complete control over their lives: 'mais surtout soumission, soumission absolue, illimitée à mes volontés [...]' (pp.166-67). Thanks to this control, she succeeds, for a time at least, in imposing on the Marquis the constancy which he failed to show in her case. But of course, fate wins in the end: the puppets she has so successfully manipulated finally take an independent course, as des Arcis becomes attached to Mademoiselle d'Aisnon (or Duquênoi).

It is clear that this story is intended to carry a lot of weight in the novel. Not only its length and the care with which it is written, but the fact that it is placed in the central episode of the journey, when Jacques and his master are held up at the inn, suggest that Diderot wants us to pay careful attention. Moreover, it is followed by the scene in which the relationship between Jacques and his master is subjected to close examination, and then by the other important story of the abbé Hudson. It is equally clear that it is not easy to interpret, and this too is surely deliberate, and very much in keeping with the problematical nature of most of the events in *Jacques le fataliste*. At first, with the surprise dénouement most recent in our memories, we might be inclined to say that it is a kind of fable telling us that however hard you try, you cannot indefinitely resist the unpredictability of life, and this would certainly be a conclusion in keeping with the general subject-matter of *Jacques*. But the surprise ending is only a small part of the story, the main body of which is concerned first with La Pommeraye's stratagem to discover the Marquis's true feelings about her, and then with her revenge.

This is the part of the story where La Pommeraye is in control, and it can be looked at for itself, as an example of human behaviour which calls for a moral judgement, or in the context of *Jacques*, as an important contribution to its total significance, that is, from an aesthetic point of view. It is the moral aspect which is taken up by the narrator (pp.197-200), when he assumes that the reader ('lecteur', not 'lectrice'!) has immediately condemned her. He points out first of all that however hateful her action may be, it is not contemptible, the more so because there is no self-interest involved. He goes on to suggest that our judgement of women is based on a rather small-minded conventional attitude. He stresses the sacrifice which she had made to the Marquis of her earlier life-style and her reputation as a woman of virtue, implying that we set much higher standards of behaviour for women than for men. Finally, if we condemn not the act of revenge itself, but the manner of it, the long-term preparation which it required, then here too we are too hasty in our judgement, since there is only a difference of degree between an immediate reaction and the careful project worked out by Madame de La Pommeraye. And the narrator ends by approving of the poetic justice implicit in condemning to marriage with a prostitute a man who has ruined a woman's reputation.

As well as being one document in the brief flowering of feminism which marked the later years of the Enlightenment, this passage is a plea for a sympathetic attitude, for a reconsideration of the conventional social criteria which usually condition our judgements. Conventional standards will almost certainly lead us to condemn La Pommeraye, as well as to take pleasure in the reversal at the end, when the tables are turned on her. Jacques's comment (p.195) that they probably turned out to be an ideal couple, is no doubt intended to echo the general reaction. But we are being told, as always in *Jacques le fataliste*, that there are other, better ways of looking at it. And the underlying truth seems to be of the same order as the comments which followed Jacques's master's knee injury: that we are unable or, in this case, disinclined to understand the sufferings of those whose problems we have not experienced.

This is one way in which the Pommeraye story, on the moral level, can be integrated into the general pattern of *Jacques le fataliste*. Other aspects of the story are best examined in conjunction with the story of the abbé Hudson (pp.220-32). With Hudson it is difficult to sympathize, although one may admire his skill and effrontery. What he shares with Madame de La Pommeraye is the power to control others, the strength of will to write his own story, using the people around him as its characters. Where he differs is that all his actions are hypocritical and motivated purely by self-interest. The story, like that of La Pommeraye, has an unexpected twist at the end, when, realizing that Richard has seen through him, he stops pretending to be a saint and says 'Mon cher Richard, vous vous foutez de moi, et vous avez raison' (p.232). But no one could suggest that this admission lessens in any way the impact of Hudson as a character; if anything, it increases it by showing that he does not really care: he is above anything that people like Richard could do to him.

The narrator makes no moral judgement on the abbé Hudson, and perhaps there is nothing to be said at this level. But if we had earlier adopted the narrator's line and limited ourselves to a moral assessment of La Pommeraye, then this story suggests that we look at it in a different light. The parallels between the two belong to the realm of aesthetic judgement: both of these characters are elevated above the common run of humanity by their capacity to make things happen; to be, at least for a time, the authors of their own destiny.

Laufer says of them: 'Madame de La Pommeraye et Hudson sont conséquents et purs. Dans un monde veule et aveugle, leur volonté de puissance crée un ordre humain, en dépit de l'irraison du destin. Leur attitude contredit le fatalisme, elle le dépasse' (*11*, pp.527-28). This is a viewpoint which suggests that La Pommeraye and Hudson are people of a different order from the other characters, whether we are speaking of Jacques and his master, or of the various episodic figures whom they meet or hear about. Hudson and La Pommeraye would thus be the only two characters who have made themselves an exception to the general rule that we are subject to the operations of destiny.

This is true enough, but another point of view would be that these two exceptional figures are simply extreme cases, test cases perhaps, of something which all the other characters want to be. Perhaps too, there is an emphasis on the moral rather than the aesthetic aspect of all these unlikely people. We may, at the narrator's instigation, feel a good deal of sympathy for Madame de La Pommeraye, but we still feel uncomfortable about what she has done, and we cannot help condemning Hudson. And how should we view Gousse if he had been successful in his plan to sue himself in order to impoverish his wife and set up house with his servant (pp.120-22)? Finally we should not forget that, as always with *Jacques*, there is probably no simple answer: one of the many themes of the book is surely the complexity of human behaviour, and the difficulty of arriving at clear-cut judgements about it. Before deciding on an interpretation we need to examine some of the other anecdotic figures and then compare them with La Pommeraye and Hudson in the context of *Jacques le fataliste* as a whole.

A short tale which might be considered as a kind of pendant to the Hudson story is that of frère Jean and Père Ange (pp.76-81). This is a story of the jealousy of Père Ange's fellow monks, who cannot tolerate the presence of an exceptionally attractive figure in their midst and successfully plot to destroy him. Leading up to the tale is the account of how frère Jean became over-zealous in his attempts to gain control of the monastery and was also outwitted by the other monks. Jean's fate was deserved, Père Ange's was not, but it is Jean who finally gets a kind of revenge by escaping with Père Ange before the other monks reduce him to madness. It is difficult to see what conclusions one can draw from this story, except perhaps that success, whether deserved or undeserved, excites envy, and disaster, if one is not stronger than those who are plotting against one. Unlike the abbé Hudson, frère Jean and Père Ange are not stronger. Another implication might be that the world cannot be relied upon to produce the rewards and punishments which we should like to think appropriate — or is it perhaps that a story should not be relied upon for this satisfaction, since we know very well that life itself is unjust?

No clear conclusion seems possible, and the same applies to many of the other stories. I have already mentioned the characters who have obsessions of one kind or another: Le Pelletier, the poet of Pondicherry, the captain and his duelling partner. To these one might add Desglands (pp.297-303), who repeatedly fights with his rival for the favour of the widow, with the result that the widow dies of grief. This is another example of absurd behaviour, made more absurd by the patch which Desglands wears on his cheek and cuts down a little each time he defeats his rival. There seems to be no moral or poetic justice in this short tale; it is simply an account of the tragic consequences of what, in other circumstances, might have been a comic obsession.

One episodic character who is explicitly introduced as an example of extraordinary behaviour is Gousse (pp.99-102; 120-22; 128-32). As the narrator says before he presents him to us: 'la nature est si variée, surtout dans les instincts et les caractères, qu'il n'y a rien de si bizarre dans l'imagination d'un poète dont l'expérience et l'observation ne vous offrissent le modèle dans la nature' (p.99). The obvious message of this is that fact is stranger than fiction, which might seem something of a platitude, but, as I have said, few of the comments made in *Jacques le fataliste* are notable for their originality when considered in isolation. Yet if we take this observation in its context, as a remark made by a narrator to a reader, it does take on a certain force. We accept the existence of someone like Gousse in life simply because there is no denying what 'l'expérience et l'observation' tell us; but we are less ready to accept such characters in fiction. The presence of Gousse, then, is another illustration of the point I discussed more fully in Chapter 2, that what we demand of a fictional work is not the truth, in the sense of verifiable facts, but what is likely, what has the 'ring of truth', in other words the 'vraisemblable'.

A further emphasis is made in the story of Gousse, however, and that is the stress laid on the total absence of moral principles in his make-up. This is what makes him so unusual. At one moment he is prepared to sell all his possessions to help a couple in difficulties, at another to add a nought to the figure on a money-order, at a third to steal books from a scholar's library (pp.101-03). 'Et prononcez après cela sur l'allure des hommes!' (p.103) the narrator concludes, challenging his reader to make sense of the way human beings behave. For Gousse is 'un original sans principes' (p.102), and this is what makes him difficult to accept, in a novel at least, if not in life.

Diderot implies during the course of the Gousse story that the reader will be reluctant to listen to it. Twice (pp.102; 103) the reader intervenes to ask for the story of Jacques again. The further implication is that we do not feel at ease with someone who is 'sans principes'. If we now look at all the stories and anecdotes, I think it is possible to say that all of the characters they portray are, in one way or another, 'sans principes', if we can take 'principes' to mean 'conventionally accepted moral standards'. Some are unprincipled in the usual sense of the word, like the abbé Hudson, and, at least as far as her individual act of revenge goes, Madame de La Pommeraye. We could also include frère Jean in this category, with his unscrupulous ambition and promiscuity. Others have principles which conflict with everyday morality or social conventions, such as an exaggerated sense of honour, like Jacques's captain, with his duelling partner and Le Pelletier (p.92), or Desglands and his rival, or else an overwhelming desire to give to others, like Le Pelletier himself, or an obsessive need to write poetry, like the poet of Pondicherry. Even Père Ange upsets the normal balance of things by drawing all the women to his confessional not because he is unusually devout, but because he is unusually attractive.

All of these characters raise social and moral problems, all are exceptional in some way. One might go on to ask whether there are any 'normal' people in *Jacques*, any characters who observe the conventions of 'vraisemblance'. The Marquis des Arcis seems normal enough to begin with, but even he ends up by making a love-match with a former prostitute, thus fitting in with the general pattern by doing something which is both unlikely and an offence to moral conventions. It would seem therefore that Diderot is implying a link between the 'vraisemblable' and the socially and morally acceptable by presenting us with a series of cases which offend against both. I do not mean to suggest that, for Diderot, the 'vraisemblable' is by definition identical with acceptable moral behaviour, but that he has chosen his examples in such a way as to suggest that our view of what is acceptable in a story is of the same order as our view of what is acceptable in society, and that both are based on a convention, not a fundamental truth. In this way he establishes a link between story-telling and our experience of life.

Earlier in this chapter I raised the question whether Madame de La Pommeraye and the abbé Hudson were characters of a different order from the other episodic figures, or simply more extreme and successful examples of the same kind of attitude. I think the answer must be a qualified 'yes' to both possibilities. This will perhaps be irritating to those who consult a critical guide for clear answers to their questions, but it would be false to Diderot's intentions to say anything else. They are of a different order in that they have crossed the barrier between subjection to fate and dominance over it: they breathe another, freer air. On the other hand they are only doing more successfully what most of the other characters have tried to do, and in this respect they raise similar moral problems. Their status is a complex one, as we should by now expect in *Jacques*, but we should remember that seeing complexity and incon-clusiveness in a work is not necessarily an admission of critical defeat. That life is complex and inconclusive is surely one of the positive messages that Diderot is trying to get across to us.

There is one further question worth asking, and that is how Jacques and his master, as characters, relate to the figures in the stories and anecdotes. Certainly they too are unusual people. Jacques's master is clearly exceptional in a negative way, though he does take on a degree of independent life as the novel proceeds. Jacques himself is obviously no ordinary servant. 'Vous avez là un serviteur qui n'est pas ordinaire' (p.215), the Marquis des Arcis remarks to Jacques's master. Even if his ideas are not his own, but taken from Spinoza *via* his capitain, he remains a thoughtful, if confused person, with acute powers of observation. This last point indicates the difference between Jacques and his master on the one hand and the episodic characters on the other. They are observers of the scene about them. It is true that Jacques often takes action in various ways, but usually this is because he is responding to the situation around him. He reacts to his environment in the way which seems most appropriate to him at the time: he is not, like the other characters, motivated by an *idée fixe*. Just as the narrator in *Jacques* stands part-way between ourselves and Jacques and his master, so Jacques and his master are intermediate figures between the narrator and the episodic stories. Not only are their characters and adventures of a different kind from those in the stories, but they have a different function in the structure of the novel. This is one point which will help to illuminate the subject of my final chapter.

5. Destiny

So many themes are present in *Jacques le fataliste*, so many problems are raised by its incidents and discussions that it is easily possible to lose sight of the fact that one of the words in its title is indeed 'fataliste'. Some of the book's most important themes, for example relationships, or moral judgements, have no self-evident links with the subject of fatalism. Even though it is possible to identify a preoccupation with fatalism at regular intervals throughout the book, it is not so easy to decide whether this is just one of the many themes or a dominant one which embraces all the others. This is one problem.

Another is to decide what exactly is meant by 'fatalism'. Does it mean, as in popular parlance, that things are meant to happen, that everything is already mapped out for us, 'écrit là-haut' in fact? Or does it mean, as some commentators have suggested, the same as 'determinism', that is, that everything that happens is subject to the laws of cause and effect, that every event is necessarily brought about by those which preceded it? Both attitudes are present in *Jacques le fataliste*, and in Jacques's own utterances. The distinction between the two has been well made by Loy (*8*, p.60): 'there is one fate or destiny which is teleological and has followed its unswerving course through all its existence; and another fate which, aiming at no foreordained endpoint, still follows an inexorable chain of causes. The first is Jacques's Great Scroll and properly referred to as Fatalism; the second may best be identified as Determinism'. These remarks are simply made to indicate that fatalism and determinism are not the same thing, but it is important not to get too obsessed with the problem: otherwise we may commit one of the cardinal sins of criticism, which is to decide what a book ought to be about and then test it to see if it is. A much more fruitful approach will be to try to understand what the text actually says in this general area, and for this we need to examine above all the actions and utterances of Jacques.

He and his master discuss the problem of fatalism at quite frequent intervals, especially during the early part of the dialogue. The clearest point that emerges from their conversations is that Jacques's belief in the fact that everything is foreordained is unshakeable: 'j'en reviens toujours au mot de mon capitaine: Tout ce qui nous arrive de bien et de mal en ce monde est écrit là-haut' (p.40). At the end of the story Jacques's opinion has not changed, so that this is one element in the book which remains constant. The objections raised by his master have no effect on him at all, not because they are not valid, but because, as Jacques says during one of their discussions: 'Prêchez tant qu'il vous plaira, vos raisons seront peut-être bonnes; mais s'il est écrit en moi ou là-haut que je les trouverai mauvaises, que voulez-vous que j'y fasse?' (p.41).

A statement like this makes further discussion impossible, and to another of his master's arguments, made from a rather different angle: whether things happen because they are written above, or whether they are written above because they happen, the answer is both final and unsatisfactory: 'Tous les deux étaient écrits l'un à côté de l'autre. Tout a été écrit à la fois. C'est comme un grand rouleau qui se déploie petit à petit [...]' (p.41). At this point the narrator intervenes to tell us that we should be grateful he is not reporting more of this discussion, since the subject has been argued about for two thousand years without anyone being further forward; and in any case, it seems, the two men 'disputaient sans s'entendre' (p.41).

These comments by the narrator raise the question whether the argument should be taken seriously. One thing is fairly obvious, both from what has been said so far and from the subsequent discussions of Jacques and his master: we are not going to discover whether Diderot believes in free-will or determinism. Given the terms of the argument and the nature of the two men who conduct it, we could not possibly expect a serious philosophical conclusion of this type to emerge. Even if we take account of the events of their journey and the various stories they tell and hear, these are too deliberately inconclusive to provide any enlightenment at this level.

Nevertheless the events, in the first place those which occur on Jacques's journey, can give us some idea of the level at which Diderot wants us to see the problem. One of the ironies of Jacques's story lies in the fact that he cannot help trying to apply his philosophy to the events in which he is involved. The absurd results of this are made clear in the incident of the brigands at the inn, which immediately follows the argument I have just discussed. Having disarmed and imprisoned the brigands, Jacques, unlike his master, is in no hurry to leave the next morning, on the grounds that they cannot know whether the situation is dangerous or not. When they do leave, he is quite content to go at a walking pace, 'toujours d'après son système' (p.44). Then it turns out that he has taken away the two keys to the rooms which contain the brigands and their clothes, and this precisely in order to gain the time which he is now losing by walking instead of trotting his horse. His explanation for this contradictory behaviour is both an unanswerable argument (for his master at least) and an admission of defeat: 'C'est que, faute de savoir ce qui est écrit là-haut, on ne sait ni ce qu'on veut ni ce qu'on fait, et qu'on suit sa fantaisie qu'on appelle raison, ou sa raison qui n'est souvent qu'une dangereuse fantaisie qui tourne tantôt bien, tantôt mal' (p.45).

There follows a lengthy reflection in which Jacques quotes his captain's views on the limited value of prudence and experience, and on our inability to assess the circumstances in which we find ourselves. 'Le calcul qui se fait dans nos têtes, et celui qui est arrêté sur le registre d'en haut, sont deux calculs bien différents. Est-ce que nous menons le destin, ou bien est-ce le destin qui nous mène?' (p.46). Once again, there is no answer to this question, but some kind of consolation is provided when a further thought of the captain's is quoted on the subject of prudence: 'et il ajoutait que la prudence ne nous assurait point un bon succès, mais qu'elle nous consolait et nous excusait d'un mauvais: aussi dormait-il la veille d'une action sous sa tente comme dans sa garnison [...]' (p.46). Here we are given a justification for calculated action, not because it will necessarily produce the right results, but because it can give us some peace of mind. Thus Jacques, unlike his master, is able to sleep peacefully at the inn after he has locked up the brigands.

The conclusions we can draw so far, then, are firstly that the question of free-will versus predestination is insoluble and only involves us in circular arguments; secondly, that our ignorance on this subject cannot prevent us from acting as if we were free; thirdly, that there is some purpose, if only a limited one, in taking the best action we can to deal with the situations which present themselves to us: at least this can affect our attitude to life even if it cannot affect the course life takes. But — and we should by now recognize this as part of the pattern of *Jacques* — any consolation or encouragement which Jacques might have drawn from his prudent action in locking up the brigands and taking away the keys now seems to be removed by the appearance of the menacing peasants. Jacques's peace of mind now turns to remorse and frustration: 'Maudites soient les clefs et la fantaisie ou la raison qui me les fit emporter! Maudite soit la prudence! etc. etc.' (p.46). That this incident turns out to be a false alarm is not so important, in this context, as the effect it has on Jacques. The point of it is surely not that he need not have bothered about being prudent, but that such conduct cannot be relied upon, either to produce the right results, or even to give the satisfaction that one has done one's best.

The whole sequence bears out the message of the 'deux calculs': there is no necessary connection between our own intentions and what is 'écrit là-haut'. Our projects, however carefully planned, and the actual course of events pursue their separate courses, sometimes coinciding, sometimes not, but without there being any way in which we can predict how things will go. But this is not a counsel of despair. People carry on behaving as if they could influence the course of events, not necessarily because they think they ought to, but because that is the way they are made, and some, like Jacques (and even more, La Pommeraye and Hudson) are better at it than others, like Jacques's master (or Gousse).

This theme, the relationship (or lack of it) between our intentions and the form our lives actually take, runs steadily through the whole of *Jacques*. A related theme, less often in evidence, is the one which is symbolized by the 'gourmette', the curb chain. For modern readers, whose lives are no longer dominated by the horse as a means of transport, it might be better to think in terms of the links in a chain. The image first occurs at the beginning of the book (p.36) as a comparison with the series of events which led from Jacques's bullet wound to his lame leg and his falling in love. It is brought up again by Jacques's master to explain the connection between buying an executioner's horse and lying unconscious at an inn (p.109). The emphasis here is on cause and effect rather than on what is 'écrit là-haut', but the purpose of these references to the 'gourmette' is not to prove that our lives are in fact determined by cause and effect but to show how the most unexpected results can come from a given cause.

The question of determinism is dealt with more directly in one of Jacques's most philosophical passages when he quotes his captain's view that 'si l'enchaînement des causes et des effets qui forment la vie d'un homme depuis le premier instant de sa naissance jusqu'à son dernier soupir nous était connu, nous resterions convaincus qu'il n'a fait que ce qu'il était nécessaire de faire' (p.217). These lines, and the passage from which they come, are the nearest we get in *Jacques* to the impression that Diderot is incorporating into it some of his materialist philosophy, a point which seems to be strengthened by the final statement: 'La distinction d'un monde physique et d'un monde moral lui semblait vide de sens' (p.218).

Passages of this kind have led some commentators (and many students) to allot them a privileged status in *Jacques*, as though, being relatively serious remarks about a very serious subject, they were the meat of the work, whereas the rest was the sauce which helped it down. To a certain extent this approach is a survival from the time when all literature was thought to address itself in a rational way to rational problems, a survival in fact from the time when *Jacques* was rejected precisely because it did not seem to fulfil these criteria. But the attempt to rehabilitate *Jacques* as a serious work because it contains *some* serious discussion, and to analyse these passages in isolation as though they carry the 'message', has been seen by most modern commentators as another way of distorting its true meaning, which can only be gathered from the work as a whole. If, trying to adopt this approach, we look at these 'serious' passages in the light of the whole story, then a possible interpretation is, to use Jacques's language, that they are there because they are 'écrits là-haut'. By this I mean that Jacques, with his belief in predestination, and his master, with his belief in freedom, will inevitably interpret life in these terms. Trying to understand life, even if it does not help us on a practical level, is still something we will do, and is therefore an integral part of our experience of life.

But such discussions, carried on in a spirit of detachment from everyday events, do not in *Jacques* thereby acquire a special status, the power to solve the problems which bother us during our active periods of involvement with life. Just as the listener to a story becomes alternately involved and detached, active and reflective, as he listens, so it is with our reactions to life. The narrator often seems to dismiss such serious observations by Jacques or his master, for example by telling us that Jacques did not in fact pursue his philosophy in his practical life (p.218), or by referring to an argument as 'ces balivernes' (p.307). This should not encourage us to go to the other extreme and dismiss them ourselves. The narrator is not Diderot, and what Diderot is saying is surely that, even if our attempts to understand life do not help us to live it, we will still continue to make them. Jacques's contradictory position is the position of us all.

Equally contradictory is the position of Jacques's master, who believes in free-will (pp.305-07). He bases this belief, among other things, on the fact that he *feels* himself to be acting freely. Jacques's answer, delayed for a number of pages, is to make him fall off his horse (pp.322-23): 'de tout ce que vous avez dit ou fait depuis une demi-heure, en avez-vous rien voulu?' Here we have an example of someone feeling free when in fact his actions were determined; the previous incident showed Jacques behaving as though he were free while *believing* himself to be determined; and the two earlier cases indicated that, whether we see things in terms of fatalism or determinism, the effect is the same: life is still full of surprises. Our own calculations and those of life follow different paths, and the effort to bring them together can only involve us in contradictions and pointless, circular arguments.

Moreover, Jacques's action in making his master fall off his horse is not that of a consistent fatalist. He invalidates his own position by the very act of trying to prove its validity. Jacques makes a claim which sets him up as a would-be substitute for fate: 'de tout ce que vous avez dit ou fait depuis une demi-heure, en avez-vous rien voulu? N'avez-vous pas été ma marionnette, et n'auriez-vous pas continué d'être mon polichinelle pendant un mois, si je me l'étais proposé?' (p.323). The only difference between Jacques and Madame de La Pommeraye is that Jacques is doing it to prove a point, whereas in La Pommeraye's case it is 'for real'. As Jacques's master says: 'Quoi! c'était un jeu?' But he was not to know this until Jacques told him. He and the Marquis des Arcis are both in the same position: unwitting victims of a plot, or a fate, of whose endpoint they are completely ignorant.

This, Diderot seems to be saying, is the condition of us all. It may be because, at times, we are victims of others; but always it is because we are victims of life. This situation is represented in *Jacques* by two symbols, the 'grand rouleau', the scroll upon which the events of our lives are written, and the 'gourmette', the chain which symbolizes the logical and unavoidable sequence of events which produces what is written. The difference between them corresponds to the difference of which I spoke earlier between fatalism and determinism, and, as is to be expected in *Jacques*, the symbols are really a statement, not about an objective reality, but about our own attitudes towards it. More exactly, they are the negative responses to the main assumptions we should like to make about life: that we are free to lead it as we want to, and that it makes sense. These are the two demands which are constantly thwarted throughout *Jacques le fataliste*. The narrator regularly reminds the reader that he is not free to hear the story he wants; Jacques's freedom of action is repeatedly limited by events, and many of the stories and anecdotes illustrate the lack of influence which human beings have over their own lives. The symbol of our ultimate powerlessness is the 'grand rouleau'.

At the same time it is quite obvious that *Jacques* does not make sense in any accepted meaning of the expression. Events follow one upon another without rhyme or reason: sometimes things turn out as the characters intended, sometimes they do not; sometimes justice is done, sometimes injustice; sometimes the reader hears what he expected to hear, sometimes not. Throughout this arbitrary sequence of events we are offered no explanation, no rationale, beyond the 'gourmette', the fact that one thing leads to another by a chain of cause and effect.

At this point it is possible to see how story-telling in *Jacques le fataliste* acts as a metaphor for life. The phrase 'écrit là-haut' is entirely appropriate for a work in which we are presented with a piece of writing, a text, and told in effect to take it or leave it, with the implication which is always present in this phrase, that we would do better to take it. This is not the spirit in which the average novel is presented to the reader. Here the novelist enters into an unspoken pact with his reader: he tries to cater for certain requirements which he assumes the reader will have: the appearance of truth, the impression that the characters are to a certain extent in control of their own destiny, and the feeling that the events which take place obey reasonable laws, the laws of 'vraisemblance'. To put it more succinctly, the average reader wants a story which appears to be true and which assumes a world where people are free and rational order prevails. *Jacques le fataliste* refuses us all of these comforts: truth is called into question by the constant appearance of exceptional people and occurrences; freedom is consistently denied; and rational order is upset by a series of unlikely coincidences and disconnected or inexplicable events.

It is not Diderot's purpose to tell us that life is like this: we know that already. If our own lives are not quite so absurd as those of Jacques and his master, we are well aware that life does not correspond to our picture of what it ought to be. What we are asked to see is what the narrator tries to make the reader see, that our expectations are unreasonable. We cannot control the complexities of life any more than the reader can expect to control the whims of the narrator. After all, the narrator is, he claims, trying to give us the truth, and this is what life does; ultimately, it is our only criterion of truth. But we have not yet exhausted the message of *Jacques*.

I said at the beginning of this chapter that there are certain themes in the book which, on the face of it, seem to have very little to do with fatalism: the urge to dominate others, relationships, the difficulty of sympathizing with other people's problems, moral judgements, and so on. One could simply say that these themes are elements in the general picture of life which Diderot is painting for us and that they should simply be accepted as part of the complexity of the whole work. This might be a reasonable attitude if it were not that our attention is deliberately drawn to these points. They all figure, as I have shown, in the discussions and reflections which interrupt the story, either as arguments between Jacques and his master or as observations made by Jacques or the narrator.

If it is possible to identify a common element in these themes, it may be that they represent the various ways in which we ourselves stand in the way of the truth, freedom and order which we want from life, and expect from the novel. The themes are very much concerned with moral problems, and perhaps the central problem is our own desire to set ourselves up in the place of fate, or to be the authors of our own story, like Madame de La Pommeraye. But La Pommeraye is only an extreme case of the various ways in which ordinary people try to assert themselves over their immediate environment, by keeping a dog, by reporting the events they have witnessed, by recounting stories, and by controlling other people. In this way, like a story-teller, we try to impose our own version of reality on the world around us.

This is where the narrator's function becomes clearer. He is in the ideal position to impose his particular version of reality upon us: he can, as he repeatedly reminds us, tell us what he likes. But he chooses not to. Instead he will give us the truth, and in doing so he reveals to us our own blindness and insensitivity. He declines to give us the comfortable feeling of order and predictability which we know we cannot get from life, if we think about it. At the same time he refuses us the surprises and excitements which, illogically, we also look for. He denies us the awareness of dignity and freedom which we should like to associate with man by showing us a world of victims, dependent on events or on other people's whims. He refuses to let us get away with an unthinking condemnation of Madame de La Pommeraye, or a simple interpretation of the problem of duelling. In general, he reminds us of the moral and physical insecurity in which we live, and implies that we have no reason to expect anything else.

All this might induce us to say, as Jacques and his captain do, that we can do nothing about fate. And so we may, if we feel so inclined. But this is not, I think, Diderot's real point. He is simply saying that, whatever discoveries we make, whatever conclusions we draw about the nature of life, we will go on behaving as we always do, just as Jacques and his master do after the revelation of their true relationship in the inn. As Jacques says: 'Croyez-vous qu'il soit inutile de savoir une bonne fois, nettement, clairement, à quoi s'en tenir?' (p.212); and perhaps this is the ambitious task which Diderot has set himself in *Jacques le fataliste*.

Two further points (from amongst many which could be made): one concerns the 'modernity' of *Jacques*, the other the attitude to life it contains and whether we should regard it as pessimistic or optimistic. *Jacques le fataliste* is often described as modern or 'before its time', and this is no doubt one of the reasons why it has aroused so much interest in recent years. Like many modern works, it flouts traditional standards of what a novel ought to be, and furthermore, as I have pointed out, it is to a large extent a reflection upon itself, a work which examines and calls into question the conditions of its own existence.

This questioning is mainly carried out by means of its complex structure, which one might call a series of receding frames. The outer frame is occupied by the narrator, who, with his reader, reflects upon the events he is recounting, and our reactions to them. Within this frame, and set back a little, is the voyage of Jacques and his master, which itself frames the story of Jacques's love-life and the reflections by the two travellers to which it gives rise. Beyond this level, framed by separate incidents in the journey, are the episodic stories, all providing new angles on the problems raised at other levels. This is a cursory and over-simplified description, but it attempts to describe the structure within which the reader constantly moves from one frame to another, so that the picture within one frame suddenly becomes the frame of another picture, and we are alternately invited to become involved in a story, or to reflect on it, or to become involved elsewhere, and so on.

This is certainly a procedure which offers close parallels with many modern novels, but it would be as well to sound a note of warning before we decide that Diderot has somehow managed to write a twentieth-century novel in the eighteenth century. It is not possible to discuss the problem fully, but it could be argued that the kind of self-conscious writing we have here is not altogether untypical of the eighteenth century. Self-parody can be found, for example in Marivaux or Voltaire; a complex structure which calls itself into question in Laclos or Sade. These are simply hints which suggest that *Jacques le fataliste* might be seen as an extreme and very successful expression of a questioning attitude about the basis of life, and writing, which was characteristic of the age.

This brings me to my other point: should we take *Jacques* as an optimistic or a pessimistic view of the human condition? I mention this because there has been a good deal of disagreement amongst critics on the subject. Some have regarded it as the expression of a kind of resigned optimism, the wisdom of Diderot's maturity; 'sagesse souriante' is a phrase often used in this context. Others see it as a gesture of failure in the face of insoluble philosophical problems. Two recent discussions of this question can be found in Cohen (*16*, pp.42-45) and in Lecointre and Le Galliot's introduction (*1*, pp.cix-cxxiv). Perhaps the way we react to this question depends, as Diderot suggests in *Jacques* that most things depend, on our temperament; but in arriving at a point of view we should take into account not only the underlying philosophy, but also the general tone of the work. To say that the book is pessimistic simply because it suggests that the main problems, both philosophical and practical, are insoluble, is not enough. After all, millions of people would agree, both now and in the eighteenth century. What is more important is the attitude Diderot invites us to take: this is certainly open to interpretation, but I think it is here that the true interest and originality of *Jacques le fataliste* lies.

Bibliographical Guide

The number of books and articles on *Jacques le fataliste* is enormous, and growing all the time. This guide is therefore selective, and aims to list the most interesting studies representing the main critical approaches.

EDITIONS

1. *Jacques le fataliste et son maître*, édition critique par Simone Lecointre et Jean Le Galliot (Paris-Geneva, Droz, 1976). This is the most recent critical edition, based on the Leningrad manuscript, which is generally regarded as the most reliable text. The introduction contains a long section devoted to the interpretation of the novel (pp.lxxxi-clxiii) which is intelligent and stimulating, sometimes difficult, and generally represents that critical view of the novel which sees it as an enquiry into the nature of the novel itself. The notes are immensely useful and informative.

2. *Jacques le fataliste*, présentation et post-face par J. Proust (Paris, Livre de Poche, 1972). This edition is worth looking at for Jacques Proust's comments.

3. *Œuvres romanesques*, édition revue par L. Pérol (Paris, Garnier, 1981). As well as *Jacques le fataliste*, this edition contains all the novels and 'contes'.

BIOGRAPHY AND GENERAL CRITICISM

4. Wilson, Arthur, *Diderot* (New York and London, Oxford University Press, 1972). The standard biography. Also contains critical comments on all Diderot's works.

5. Kempf, Roger, *Diderot et le roman, ou le démon de la présence* (Paris, Seuil, 1964). A stimulating and original study of Diderot as a novelist.

6. Mylne, Vivienne, *The Eighteenth-Century French Novel: Techniques of Illusion* (Manchester University Press, 1965; revised edition, Cambridge University Press, 1981). An intelligent and reliable study of the French novel throughout the period.

7. Showalter, English, *The Evolution of the French Novel, 1641-1782* (Princeton University Press, 1972). A full account of the development of the French novel as a vehicle of realism.

STUDIES OF JACQUES LE FATALISTE

8. Loy, Robert, *Diderot's Determined Fatalist: a Critical Appreciation of Jacques le fataliste* (New York, King's Crown Press, Columbia University, 1950). The first full-length study of the book, with much sensible and perceptive comment.

9. Crocker, Lester, '*Jacques le fataliste*: an 'expérience morale'', *Diderot Studies*, III (1961), pp.73-99. A frequently quoted article which interprets *Jacques* as an examination of moral problems.

10. May, Georges, 'Le maître, la chaîne et le chien dans *Jacques le fataliste*', *Cahiers de l'Association Internationale des Etudes Françaises*, 13 (1961) pp.269-82. An excellent study of Diderot's use of various themes and motifs.

11. Laufer, Roger, 'La structure et la signification de *Jacques le fataliste*', *Revue des Sciences Humaines*, 112 (1963), pp.517-35. One of the first studies to concentrate primarily on the structure of the work.

12. Smiétanski, Jacques, *Le Réalisme dans 'Jacques le fataliste'* (Paris, Nizet, 1965). An interesting, but now much disputed study of *Jacques*.

13. Pruner, Francis, *L'Unité secrète de 'Jacques le fataliste'* (Paris, Minard, 1970). A controversial study on the hidden message of *Jacques*. Contains a number of interesting insights.

14. Roelens, Maurice, '*Jacques le fataliste* devant la critique contemporaine', *Dix-huitième siècle*, 5 (1973), pp.119-36. An excellent survey of critical reactions up to 1973, with some suggestions on further approaches to interpretation.

15. Werner, Stephen, *Diderot's Great Scroll: Narrative Art in 'Jacques le fataliste'*, *Studies on Voltaire and the Eighteenth Century*, 128 (Oxford, Voltaire Foundation, 1975). An impressive study which sees *Jacques* as marking a turning-point in eighteenth-century values. Needs careful reading.

16. Cohen, Huguette, *La Figure dialogique dans 'Jacques le fataliste'*, *Studies on Voltaire and the Eighteenth Century*, 162 (Oxford, Voltaire Foundation, 1976). Another very interesting interpretation, this time mainly from the point of view of the structure of the novel.

17. O'Gorman, Donal, 'Hypotheses for a new reading of *Jacques le fataliste*', *Diderot Studies*, 19 (1978), pp.129-43. A controversial and highly interesting theory about the significance of Jacques and his master.

18. Baudiffier, Serge, 'La parole et l'écriture dans *Jacques le fataliste*', *Studies on Voltaire and the Eighteenth Century*, 185 (Oxford, Voltaire Foundation, 1980), pp.283-95. A difficult but rewarding study of the significance Diderot attached to the conversational form of *Jacques*.

19. Walter, Eric, '*Jacques le fataliste' de Diderot* (Paris, Hachette, 1975). An excellent and concise coverage of all the chief critical problems in *Jacques*. Not intended as an introductory study.

CRITICAL GUIDES TO FRENCH TEXTS

edited by

Roger Little, Wolfgang van Emden, David Williams